Contents

Part 1

★★★★★★★★★★★★★★★★★★★★★★★★★★★★★★

The South after the Civil War

1 Former slaves and their memories

In December 1865 the United States Congress passed a law making slavery illegal. Over the next few years the Federal Government ordered that the newly freed blacks were to have equal citizenship with whites, including the right to vote.

Most of the freed slaves wanted to get away from the plantations. Thousands wandered around looking for work but these first years of freedom were hard. Many died of starvation in the harsh winter of 1866–7. Their former masters rarely gave them land to own and made life difficult for blacks who wanted to claim their right to vote. The period 1865–77 was the time of 'Reconstruction', when the defeated South was under military rule from the North and some Northern leaders hoped to reconstruct, or rebuild, a more equal society. But did Reconstruction work? Some of the slaves freed in 1865 were still alive between 1937 and 1938 when government researchers, led by a man called Bernard Botkin, toured the South interviewing them about their memories of Reconstruction. Martha Dixon and Warren McKinney, the ex-slaves whose experiences are recorded here, were both in their eighties when they were interviewed in 1937.

A Martha Dixon

The slaves heard the news of freedom in different ways – some earlier, some later, some secretly, but all hopefully. 'Everybody talk 'bout freedom and hope to git free 'fore they die.'

Being free as a jay bird or a toad frog, as they said, they obeyed the first impulse, which was one of flight or movement. Some were gone before the master was half-way through telling them they were free. Others went off and came back because they 'didn't have no place to go and nothing to eat'.

The masters too, reacted to freedom in different ways. Some said 'You all go on away. . . . You have to look out for yourselves now'. Others said: 'Go if you wants, and stay if you wants.' Some gave their Negroes a small piece of land to work. 'But the mostest of them never give 'em nothing; a heap lot of the marses got raging mad, they shot niggers down by the hundreds.'

'It seem like the white people can't git over us being free and they do everything to hold us down all the time. We don't git no schools for a long time; and we can't go round where they have the voting, unless we want to catch a whipping some night and we have to keep bowing and scraping when we are round white folks like we did when we was slave. . . .'

From B. A. Botkin (ed.), *Lay My Burden Down*, University of Chicago Press, 1958.

2

B Warren McKinney

I was born in Edgefield County, South Carolina. I was born a slave of George Strauter. My ma was a slave in the field. I was eleven years old when freedom was declared. When I was little, Mr. Strauter whipped my ma. It hurt me as it did her. I hated him. She was crying. I chucked rocks at him.

When the war close, Ma took her four children bundled 'em up and went to Augusta. The government give out rations there. My ma washed and ironed. People died in piles. They said it was the change of living. Some said it was cholera and some took consumption. Several families had to live in one house.

The reconstruction was a mighty hard time. Me and ma couldn't live. A man paid our ways to Carlisle, Arkansas and we came. We started working for Mr. Emerson. He had a big store, teams and land. We liked it fine and I been here fifty-six years now. There was so much wild game, living was not so hard. If a fellow could get a little bread and a place to stay, he was all right. After I came to this state, I voted some; I have farmed and worked at odd jobs.

From B. A. Botkin (ed.), *Lay My Burden Down*, University of Chicago Press, 1958.

Questions

1 What grievances did the blacks have about their treatment by the whites in the first years of freedom?

2 Why was it 'the first impulse' of many ex-slaves to move away from the plantation as soon as they were freed?

3 What words and expressions in Martha Dixon's way of speaking are still commonly used in the Southern states of the USA?

4 Can you find examples in the extracts of how whites felt about giving full citizenship to blacks?

5 Is there any evidence in these two accounts to suggest that Reconstruction brought much improvement to the lives of ex-slaves?

6 Why do you think food would be rationed in the South just after the Civil War?

7 How old was Warren McKinney in 1937? How could you find out whether his memory of Reconstruction could be relied upon?

2 The Ku Klux Klan

After the Civil War, a Confederate general, Nathan Forrest, founded the society known as the Ku Klux Klan. Its purpose was to terrorise all black people who demanded rights such as owning their own land or voting in elections and to frighten off any white person who seemed to support them. The Klan often used violence and many blacks were lynched – or hanged without a proper trial. In some places a favourite Klan target was the local school, opened to give ex-slaves and their children a chance to be educated.

In these extracts ex-slaves interviewed in 1937 tell the government researchers led by Bernard Botkin about their experiences with the Klan. All three were in their eighties when they were interviewed.

A Ben Johnson, North Carolina

I will never forgit when they hung Cy Guy. They hung him for a scandalous insult to a white woman, and they comed after him a hundred strong.

They tries him there in the woods, and they scratches Cy's arm to git some blood, and with that blood they writes that he shall hang 'tween the heavens and the earth till he am dead, dead, dead and that any nigger what takes down the body shall be hunged too . . .

From B. A. Botkin (ed.), *Lay My Burden Down*, University of Chicago Press, 1958.

B Pierce Harper, North Carolina

After us colored folk was 'sidered free and turned loose, the Klu Klux broke out. Some colored people started to farming. If they got so they made good money the Klu Klux would come and murder 'em. The government builded schoolhouses and the Klu Klux went to work and burned 'em down.

After the Klu Kluxes got so strong, the colored men got together and made the complaint before the law. The governor told the law to give 'em the old guns in the armoury, what the Southern soldiers had used, so they issued the colored men old muskets and said protect themselves. They'd hide in the cabins and then's when they found out who a lot of them Klu Kluxes was, cause a lot of 'em was kilt. The Klu Kluxes wore long sheets and covered the hosses with sheets. Men you thought was your friend was Klu Kluxes.

From B. A. Botkin (ed.), *Lay My Burden Down*, University of Chicago Press, 1958.

C Brawley Gilmore, South Carolina

John Good, a darky blacksmith, used to shoe the horses for the Klu Klux. He would mark the horseshoe with a bent nail or something like that. They suspicioned John; they kept him in hiding, and when he told them his tricks they killed him.

From B. A. Botkin (ed.), *Lay My Burden Down*, University of Chicago Press, 1958.

D White terrorism

From *Harper's Weekly*, 1873

The White League was a secret society which flourished in Louisiana and other Southern states between 1867 and 1877. It used terror tactics to stop blacks gaining any benefits from the Reconstruction period.

Questions

1 How does the first extract show the way in which the Klan took the law into its own hands?

2 In what two ways did the Klan try to stop ex-slaves from taking up benefits of freedom?

3 Why do you think the governor of North Carolina gave the blacks weapons to defend themselves rather than trying to arrest members of the Ku Klux Klan?

4 What did Brawley Gilmore mean when he said 'They suspicioned John'?

5 Why would Klan members try to prevent blacks being educated?

6 Do you think the cartoon is supporting the blacks or the Ku Klux Klan? Give reasons for your answer.

7 Which grievances of the blacks are illustrated in the cartoon?

3 The United States in the 1890s

The map and photographs suggest just a few of the changes that took place in the thirty years after the Civil War.

The slave-owning states which made up the Confederacy are shaded. There were four other slave-owning states which stayed with the Union: Delaware, Maryland, Kentucky and Missouri. West Virginia was made a state in the Union after the district broke away from the Confederacy.

Part Two of this book deals with the settlement of the West. The dates for newly formed states give clues about the timing and direction of the westward movement. The first railway to cross the continent is shown on the map as it played an important part in the settlement. By the time it was built there was a complicated network of railways in the eastern USA.

Part Three tells the story of the millions of newcomers who entered the USA from Europe. Most of them never reached the western farming states. They stayed to swell the industrial cities such as Chicago or Pennsylvania. Many got no further than New York. Scenes like that in photograph C could be found in cities in many parts of the country.

A The United States in 1890

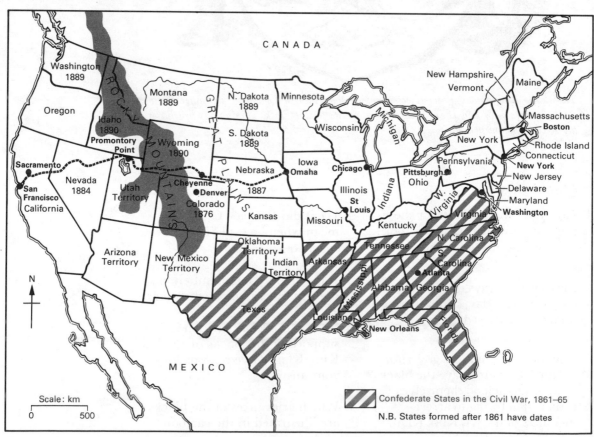

Confederate States in the Civil War, 1861–65

N.B. States formed after 1861 have dates

B Louisiana

Cotton pickers in Louisiana in about 1900.

C New York

New York City in the late 1890s. The Jewish market in Hester Street.

Questions

1 Name the five Great Lakes shown between the USA and Canada.

2 Name the three rivers shown on the map.

3 Using the scale to help you, work out the distance between New York and San Francisco and from the Canadian border to New Orleans.

4 Make your own map to show the Confederate States (shaded on this map) and the Union States (all those formed before 1861).

5 Which areas were still territories and not states in 1890?

6 Why are some state borders straight lines and others not?

7 (a) What does the photograph of Louisiana tell you about life in the Deep South thirty years after the Civil War?

(b) What changes might the old man in the picture have seen in his lifetime?

(c) Are there any ways in which photograph B adds to the information in Sources 1 and 2?

8 (a) What does photograph C suggest about living conditions for many immigrants living in New York?

(b) What signs are there in this photograph that New York was already an overcrowded city?

Part 2

★★★★★★★★★★★★★★★★★★★★★★★★★★★

The West

4 Railway journey from coast to coast

Before 1860 the railways (which the Americans call railroads) went only as far as the Mississippi and Missouri rivers on their way westwards from the large eastern cities. By May 1869, the United States had its first railroad crossing from coast to coast.

The steam locomotives gave a great opportunity for settlers to move on to the cattle and farm lands of the West. Rich businessmen could afford to travel in the sleeping cars designed by George M. Pullman.

The Union Pacific Railway Company built the line westwards from Omaha, whilst the Central Pacific built the line eastwards from San Francisco to meet it at Promontory Point in the state of Utah (see map on page 6).

In this extract, a traveller named West describes his experiences crossing the American continent by rail in 1869.

A Memories of a traveller

The traveller bound for the Far West starts from New York in the evening by the Pacific Express and on the morning of the following day arrives at Rochester where Pullman palace-cars are attached to the train. No royal personage can be more comfortably housed than the occupant of a Pullman car, provided the car be a hotel one.

The hotel car is divided into sections forming state rooms where parties of four can be accommodated. Between these rooms seats are arranged in the usual way. At the rear is a kitchen which contains every appliance. The passengers in the other cars must rush out when the refreshment station is reached and hastily swallow an ill-cooked meal.

Having reached Chicago one must change to catch the Pacific coast train. . . . On reaching Omaha confusion reigned supreme as at most American railroad stations. Excited passengers were rushing about in quest of baggage which is often going astray.

Those who got this part of their business over proceeded to the office to secure berths in the Pullman sleepers. The prospect of spending several nights in an ordinary carriage is enough to depress the mind and daunt the courage of the hardiest traveller . . .

The first real sensation is obtained at Jackson, a small station a hundred miles [160 kilometres] from Omaha. Here many of the passengers see genuine Indians for the first time. They are Pawnees and we are

From W. F. Rae, *Westward by Rail*, London, 1870.

told they are friendly, being supported by the Government. At Grand Island station the traveller is told he may bid goodbye to schools and churches and keep his eye peeled for buffalo. The event of the succeeding morning was halting at Cheyenne for breakfast which was antelope steaks.

Promontory is the western terminus of the Union Pacific and the eastern terminus of the Central Pacific. Passengers have to change cars, secure fresh sleeping berths and get their baggage moved. The morning after leaving Elko there was a commotion – the engine and tender had been thrown off the rails in a collision with a herd of cattle.

The engine driver ran extra risks to make up the time lost and the descent from Summit Station to Sacramento was made with exceptional rapidity. Glad though all were to reach Sacramento, not a few were exceptionally thankful to have reached it with whole limbs.

Questions

1 Look at the map on page 6 and find the places mentioned in the extract.

2 Work out the distance by rail between New York and Sacramento.

3 'Promontory is the western terminus of the Union Pacific and the eastern terminus of the Central Pacific.' Explain the meaning and importance of this sentence.

4 What sort of railway car did the writer of this extract travel in? Does this tell you anything about his background?

5 How many times did the writer change cars during the journey?

6 How did the government support Indians so that they became friendly?

7 Imagine you had been a passenger in an 'ordinary carriage' on the journey between New York and Sacramento. Write a letter to the railway company complaining about all the things which went wrong on your journey.

8 Explain how the railways would have benefited each of the following: immigrants, farmers, businessmen.

9 Draw a poster from a railway company encouraging immigrants to use the railway.

5 Cattle country and cowboys

Before the 1880s many millions of cattle roamed free on the plains of Texas. They were driven to the railroad junctions in Kansas and Nebraska by the cowboys. Many of these cowboys were former Confederate soldiers who had drifted West after the Civil War. By the 1890s the cattle drives had come to an end as the trails were blocked by settlers' farms and ranches.

In the extract below, written in 1888, Theodore Roosevelt, a great lover of the outdoor life, describes the cattle country and its cowboys. Roosevelt was himself a rancher in the years before he became President and he knew well the day-to-day routine of a ranch cowboy.

A Theodore Roosevelt

The great grazing lands of the West lie in what is known as the arid belt; it includes New Mexico, part of Arizona, Colorado, Wyoming, Montana and the Western portions of Texas, Kansas, Nebraska and the Dakotas. The whole region is one vast stretch of grazing country, with only here and there spots of farm land.

It is a region of light rainfall; there is no timber except along the beds of streams. The level, seemingly endless plains are sometimes broken by abrupt hills usually bare, but often clad with a dense growth of dwarfed pines.

In stock-raising regions there are usually few towns; on the other hand, wealthy cattlemen, like miners, always spend their money freely, and accordingly towns like Denver and Cheyenne are far pleasanter places than cities of five times their population in the states to the east.

In the cattle towns the cowboys gallop their wiry little horses down the street, their lithe, supple figures erect or swaying slightly as they sit loosely in the saddle. They are smaller and less muscular than the wielders of axe and pick; but they are as hardy and self-reliant as any men who ever breathed – with bronzed set faces and keen eyes. Their appearance is picturesque with their jingling spurs, the big revolvers stuck in their belts and bright silk handkerchiefs loosely round their necks over the open collars of the flannel shirts.

When drunk they cut mad antics, riding their horses into saloons and indulging too often in deadly shooting affrays; but except while on such sprees they are quiet rather self-contained men. They are much better fellows than small farmers and agricultural labourers, nor are the mechanics and workers in the big cities to be mentioned in the same breath.

Some of the cowboys are Mexicans, who generally do the work well enough, but are not trustworthy. Moreover they are regarded with extreme disfavor by the Texans in an outfit. Southern born whites will not work under Mexicans and look down upon all colored and half-caste races.

From Theodore Roosevelt, *Cattle Country of the Far West*, Charles Scribner's Sons, 1925.

B Bill Pickett, a black cowboy star

Bill Pickett – a star attraction on the Wild West Show circuit for about fifteen years in the period before World War One.

Questions

1 Why does Theodore Roosevelt say that places like Denver and Cheyenne are far pleasanter than larger cities in the east? Pick out the words in the extract which tell you that cattle towns were very 'lively'.

2 What evidence is there in Source A to suggest that the writer admired the cowboys and their way of life?

3 What phrases in the passage suggest that the cattle lands were lawless places?

4 What is Roosevelt's opinion of Mexican cowboys? What facts or figures would you need to see whether he was correct?

5 About one in three cowboys was black. Can you suggest why so many blacks became cowboys?

6 Very few films or novels about the West mention blacks. Can you suggest any reasons for this?

7 Imagine that Bill Pickett's Wild West Show is coming to town. Write and illustrate a poster advertising the show. Sources 7 and 8 will help you decide who the other characters in the show might be.

6 Moving West, 1884

The Homestead Act of 1862 said that all American adults, except those who had fought against the government, could claim 160 acres (about 65 hectares) of land for virtually nothing, once they had farmed it for five years.

Hundreds of thousands of people travelled vast distances west by railroad or covered wagon to settle on a homestead on the open plains. Their first homes were usually built from blocks of turf and called 'soddies'. The roof was supported by timber frames whilst the insides were often plastered with sand and clay. Sometimes homes were 'dug-outs' made by digging a simple 'cave' in the side of a hill.

One family who moved West were the O'Kieffes who settled in Nebraska in 1884. Charley O'Kieffe, a young boy at the time, kept an account of his family's adventures in their new home. The following extract is taken from the diary which he wrote between the years 1884 and 1898.

A   The O'Kieffe family

On September 15th, 1884, about ten in the morning, our covered wagon moved out on a journey [to Nebraska] which was to require six weeks and cover five hundred or more miles [over 800 kilometres], including detours.

The O'Kieffes taking part in this exodus were Mother, brother Ira, fourteen; sister Minnie, nine; brother George, about seven; and myself five – seen but not heard very much. Of our worldly goods, the heavier and more bulky stuff – farm implements, household effects, sewing machine, family records, Bible and pictures – had been loaded onto an immigrant car to be shipped by rail to our destination. The less cumbersome things were stowed away in the bottom of our wagon.

The new life
City people, when they talk about neighbors, usually mean folks across the street or next door; but in a farming or ranching area nearness is measured in terms of miles. Seeing a neighbor – or seeing anybody as far as that goes was certainly not something that happens every day.

Folks lived in crude homes, mostly soddies with here and there a dug out. Nearly every item in the house, with the possible exception of a favorite rocking chair or desk brought along on the trip west, was homemade out of native lumber. . . .

Rushville, the nearest town
One of the grandest of the older men was William Alexander, who owned the biggest and best store in town. There was the day I walked home for supper with his beautiful daughter Mary and had the unusual experience of drinking out of real glassware, eating off real china plates with real silverware, and, for the first time in my life, using a linen table napkin.

From Charley O'Kieffe, *Western Story: The Recollections of Charley O'Kieffe 1884–1898*, University of Nebraska, 1974.

B Settlers in Dakota

A family of settlers in Dakota, photographed in 1885.

Questions

1 What is the house in the photograph made out of?

2 How far did the O'Kieffe family travel on average in a day?

3 Why do you think the wagons had to make some detours?

4 What do you think were the more precious items that the family took west with them? Give reasons for your answer.

5 What was 'native lumber'?

6 Using Source A and the map on page 6, can you suggest from where the O'Kieffe family might have started? How could you check whether your answer was correct?

7 Make a list of the sort of luxuries a family of settlers might have had to do without.

8 How does the photograph support the information that you have been given in the extract?

9 Which of the goods in the photograph would have been brought west by the family?

7 A quiet frontier heroine

During the nineteenth century about 30 million people left their homes in Europe to seek a new life in the United States. Some 10 million travelled before the Civil War began in 1861. They came mainly from Ireland, Great Britain, Germany and Norway. Huge advertising campaigns, particularly by railway companies, encouraged these immigrants to move westwards.

Guri Endresen was a Norwegian immigrant who settled in Minnesota State. When a party of Santee Sioux Indians attacked her farm in summer 1862 Guri rescued two injured men from another farm and took them and her surviving family to a settlement nearly 50 kilometres away. Four years later she moved back to her home district and wrote to her mother in Norway explaining what had happened.

A Letter from Guri Endresen, 2 December 1866

I have received your letter of April 14, this year, and I send you my heartiest thanks for it, for it gives me great happiness to hear from you and to know that you are alive, well and in general thriving.

From R. Hoff, *America's Immigrants*, Henry Z. Walck Inc., 1967.

Gin and Britha were carried off by the wild Indians, but they got a chance the next day to make their escape. I myself wandered aimlessly around on my land with my youngest daughter, and I had to look while they shot my precious husband dead and in my sight my dear son Ole was shot through the shoulder. But he got well from this wound and lived a little more than a year. We also found my oldest son Endre shot dead but I did not see the firing of this shot. For two days and nights I hovered about here with my little daughter, between fear and hope and almost crazy before I found my wounded son and a couple of other persons unhurt, who helped us to get away. But God be thanked, I kept my life and my sanity, though all my movable property was torn away and stolen. But this would have been nothing if only I could have had my loved husband and children – but what shall I say? God permitted it to happen thus and I have to accept my heavy fate and thank Him for having spared my life and those of some of my children.

I must also let you know my daughter Gjaertru has land, received from the Government under a law called 'The Homestead Law' and for a quarter section of land they pay 16 dollars and after five years they receive a deed and complete possession of the property. My daughter Guri is in house service for an American about a hundred miles [160 kilometres] from here.

I must also remark that it was four years August 21 since that I had to flee from my dear home, and since that time I have not been on my land, there are now only ruins left as reminders of the terrible Indians. Still I moved up here to the neighborhood again this summer. A number of families have moved back here again. I am now staying at the home of Sjur Anderson, two and a half miles [4 kilometres] from home.

B Escapees from the Sioux

Escapees photographed during the Sioux uprising in Minnesota, 21 August 1862.

Questions

1 What does the letter tell you about the sort of person Guri Endresen was?

2 Why might the Indians have attacked the Endresen farm and other farms in the country?

3 Does Guri show any understanding of the effects of homesteading on the Indians?

4 Guri settled in Minnesota State where there were many Norwegian immigrants. Why do many immigrant groups keep together in a 'new' country?

5 What particular difficulties might frontier women have had to endure? (Remember farms were often a long distance apart.)

6 What sort of things do you think might be in the wagons at the left of the photograph?

7 What are the two men at the back of the group holding up in the air?

8 The Indians' Voice

Through the 1860s settlers and the United States Cavalry pushed the Indians back on to the Great Plains between the Mississippi River and the Rocky Mountains. By the 1890s the Great Plains could no longer support large numbers of Indians because of the disappearance of the buffalo. Millions of buffalo were slaughtered by railway construction crews and professional hunters such as 'Buffalo Bill'. As time went on, more and more Indians were forced to live on restricted areas of land known as reservations.

Here, two chiefs complain about their people's treatment by the white men. Plenty Coups describes the pressure on the Indian way of life and Luther Standing Bear remembers how children were forced to attend schools set up by the white men.

A Plenty-Coups (1848–1932) – Chief of the Crow Tribe

By the time I was forty, I could see our country was changing fast. Anybody could see that soon there would be no buffalo on the plains and everybody was wondering how we could live after they were gone. . . .

Their houses [the white men's] were near the water holes and their villages on the rivers. We made up our minds to be friendly with them but we found this difficult because the white men too often promised to do one thing and then did another.

They spoke very loudly when they said their laws were made for everybody; but we learned that although they expected us to keep them, they thought nothing of breaking them themselves. They told us not to drink whisky, yet they made it, and traded it to us for furs and robes until both were nearly gone. Their wise ones said we might have their religion, but when we tried to understand it we found out there were too many kinds of religion among white men.

From Plenty-Coups, *Plenty-Coups, Crow Chief 1848–1932*, New York World Books, 1932.

B Luther Standing Bear (1868–1938) – Chief of the Lakota (Sioux) Tribe

Our first resentment was in having our hair cut. If the argument that has been advanced is true, that the children needed delousing, why were not girls as well as boys put through the same process?

Our second resentment was against trousers. Our bodies were used to constant bathing in the sun, air and rain and the function of the pores of our skin was at once stopped by trousers of heavy sweat absorbing material aided by that worst of all torments – red flannel underwear. Many times we have been laughed at for our native way of dressing, but could anything we ever wore compare in utter foolishness to the steel ribbed corset and the huge bustle which our girls adopted after a few years in school?

The Indian, essentially an outdoor person, had no use for the handkerchief, he was practically immune to colds. To clothe a man falsely is only to distress his spirit and to make him ridiculous. My plea to the American Indian is to retain his tribal dress.

From Luther Standing Bear, *Land of the Spotted Eagle*, Houghton Mifflin Co., 1933.

C Indian snake dancers

Indian snake dancers perform for fashionably dressed tourists in 1902.

Questions

1 What was the value of the buffalo to the Indians and to the white man?

2 List and compare the complaints made against Indians in Source 7A with the Indian complaints against white men in these two extracts.

3 Can you explain why Americans wanted Indians to dress and behave like people who had come to the USA from Europe?

4 Why might the Indian dancers in the photograph have felt self-conscious or degraded?

5 What do you think the well-dressed tourists in the picture might be thinking?

Part 3

★★★★★★★★★★★★★★★★★★★★★★★★★★★★★★

New people, new work, 1865–1918

9 The story of a self-made man

Andrew Carnegie had come to the United States from Scotland with his family at the age of twelve. At first he helped his father doing hand-loom weaving at home and then followed him into factory work. In this extract from his autobiography, Andrew Carnegie describes how he set out on the climb from poor factory hand to rich businessman. Later he owned America's first steel plant and by 1900 his income was estimated to be $20 million a year.

A Andrew Carnegie

My father found it necessary to give up hand-loom weaving, and to enter the cotton factory of Mr. Blackstock, an old Scotsman in Allegheny City, where we lived. In this factory he also obtained for me a position, and my first work was done there at 1 dollar and twenty cents per week. In the winter father and I had to rise and breakfast in the darkness, reach the factory before daylight, and, with a short interval for lunch, work till after dark. I took no pleasure in the work; but every cloud has a silver lining, as it gave me the feeling that I was doing something for our family. I have made millions since, but none of those millions gave me such happiness as my first week's earnings.

Soon after this John Hay, a fellow Scot manufacturer of bobbins in Allegheny City, needed a boy. I went and received two dollars a week. I had to run a small steam engine and fire the boiler in the cellar of the bobbin factory. I found myself night after night sitting up in bed fearing that the boiler might burst.

My parents had their own troubles. I must play the man and bear mine. I looked every day for some change to take place. One day the chance came. Mr. Hay had to make out some bills. He had no clerk and was himself a poor penman. He gave me some writing to do.

One evening in 1850 I was told that Mr. David Brooks, manager of the telegraph office, wanted a messenger for two and a half dollars a week. Father and I walked over from Allegheny to Pittsburgh, a distance of nearly two miles [3.2 kilometres].

I was dressed in my one white linen shirt and my Sunday suit; I had at that time but one linen suit of summer clothing, and every Saturday night my mother washed these clothes and ironed them, and I put them on fresh on Sabbath morning. There was nothing that Leroine [his mother] did not do in the struggle we were making for elbow room in the Western world. [The interview was successful.]

From Andrew Carnegie, *The Autobiography of Andrew Carnegie*, Houghton Mifflin Co., 1920.

B   Factory life

An engraving of 1868 by Winslow Homer showing workers leaving a factory.

Questions

1   Why was Andrew Carnegie so pleased about his first week's wage packet?

2   Where do you think Carnegie learnt to read and write?

3   From this extract, and Sources 10 and 11, can you suggest reasons why many Americans admired men like Carnegie?

4   Look at Source B. Do you think the artist was for or against life in this New England factory?

5   Look at the ten or twelve people at the front of the picture. Do they provide any clues about the different types of people who worked in such factories? What might the workers be carrying in their cans?

10 Lower East Side, New York

Between 1880 and 1920 millions of immigrants entered the United States. Nearly 40 per cent of them came from Poland, Western Russia or from Eastern European areas such as Bohemia (now part of Czechoslovakia). The new immigrants met with a great deal of hostility, partly on religious grounds as most of them were not Protestants but Jews, Catholics or Orthodox Christians.

Large numbers of immigrants from Southern China also entered the United States during these years. They and the Europeans were crowded into the poorer parts of big cities such as Chicago and New York.

This is an eye-witness account of the Bowery district in the Lower East Side of New York City, where many of the immigrants lived. It was written in about 1898.

A The Bowery

The Bowery was probably at its gayest between 1880 and 1900 'The livest [liveliest] mile on the face of the earth'. More and more saloons . . . dance halls and dives came to crowd out legitimate business.

A short alley in the Fourth Ward [local electoral district] in 1885 had 140 families living on it, of whom 100 were Irish, 38 Italian and 2 German. It was typical of lower New York.

A huge Italian quarter was growing up west of the Bowery, along Mulberry and Mott Streets. The Jews were dotting the Bowery, Baxter, Division, Grand and other streets with their favorite businesses – clothing, jewelry, pawnbroking. They came in increasing numbers from Russia and Poland, filling the tenements of Bayard and Hester; stocking every tenement backyard with chickens, which, spasmodically cleaned out by indignant police, promptly came back again. They were slowly crowding out the old German and English inhabitants.

Crowded in between the Italians and Chatham Square that strange exotic community, Chinatown, was growing rapidly. In 1872 there were 12 Chinamen in the neighborhood and by 1880 a Chinese village of 700 had almost taken possession of two short streets, Pell and Doyers, and of two blocks of Mott Street. Most of the inhabitants still wore the pigtail, silken blouse, baggy trousers, and thick-soled shoes of the old country.

More immigrants were coming than industry could decently support and in the crowded slums many of them were driven to desperate toil to keep soul and body together; Jews laboring day and night on trousers at a dollar a dozen pairs; Bohemians rolling cigars in their tenements at nearly 4 dollars per thousand and a man and wife, by working 6 a.m. to 9 p.m. might earn nearly 12 dollars per week. The children of such families began working as soon as their little fingers could master a detail; or they became newsboys, or bootblacks, or vagabonds of the streets, living by begging or prostitution.

From Alvin H. Harlow, *Old Bowery Days; The Chronicles of a Famous Street*, New York & London, 1931.

B Lower East Side, 1890

Key

1 Lavanburg Homes
2 Bed Linens Market
3 Orchard Street
  Pushcart Market
4 Henry Street
  Settlement Playhouse
5 Amalgamated
  Dwellings
6 Henry Street
  Settlement
7 Educational Alliance
8 Jewish Daily
  Forward
9 Division Street
  Shopping Center
10 Knickerbocker
  Village
11 Oldest House in
  Manhattan
12 Franklin Square
13 Spanish-Portuguese
  Cemetery
14 Columbus Park
  Mulberry Bend
15 Olliffe Pharmacy
16 Secondhand Clothing
  Market
17 Manhattan Bridge
  Plaza
18 Bowery Outdoor
  Jewelry Market
19 Mott Street Pushcart
  Market
20 Police Headquarters
21 'Thieves' Market'
22 Salvation Army
  Hotel
23 Bowery Mission

Questions

1 How many different immigrant groups are mentioned in Source A?

2 What evidence is there in the extract to suggest that these immigrant groups tended to keep together in New York?

3 Can you suggest some possible reasons why these immigrants left their homelands to come to the United States?

4 What is a pawnbroker? Why are they usually found in the poorer districts of cities and towns?

5 Using the extract and map to help you, can you suggest any reasons why some Americans

disliked, and even hated, these 'new' immigrants?

6 Why do you think the sort of jobs described in the last paragraph of Source A came to be known as 'sweated labour'?

7 Which groups of workers mentioned in the extract might have lived in Knickerbocker Village?

8 Make a simple but larger copy of the map and, using Source A to help you, mark the areas inhabited by the different immigrant groups. Use different colours to represent each immigrant group.

11 Immigrants in the city

The 28 million immigrants who settled in the United States between 1860 and 1920 came with little money and were prepared to take up jobs with low wages. Many came from farming areas in Europe and were unskilled in industrial trades.

Louis Adamic came to the United States in 1913 from Slovenia, now part of Yugoslavia but then ruled by Austria. Rocco Corresca was an Italian immigrant, who came to America with his brother in the early part of this century and took a labouring job. After two years the brothers owned shoe-shine parlours and looked forward to the day when they would become American citizens with full voting rights.

A Louis Adamic

My notion of the United States was that it was a grand, amazing, somewhat fantastic place – the Golden Country – huge beyond conception, untellably exciting.

In America one could make pots of money in a short time, acquire immense holdings, wear a white collar and have polish on one's boots – and eat white bread, soup and meat on week days as well as on Sundays, even if one were but an ordinary workman to begin with.

I heard a returned Americanec* tell of regions known as Texas and Oklahoma where single farms – ranches he called them – were larger than a whole province of Slovenia. In America even the common people were 'citizens' not 'subjects', as they were in the Austrian Empire and in most European countries.

From Louis Adamic, *Laughing in the Jungle*, Harper & Bros, 1932.

*Someone who had returned to Slovenia from the USA

B Rocco Corresca

...We went to Newark and got work on the street. We paid a man five dollars for getting us the work and after six months we had nearly 200 dollars saved.... Plenty of the men spoke English and they taught us, and we taught them to read and write Italian. That was at night for we had a lamp in our room and there were only five other men who lived in that room with us.

We got up at half past five in the morning and made coffee on the stove and had a breakfast of bread and cheese, onions, garlic and red herrings. We got from the butcher the meat that other people would not buy, but they don't know what is good...

From Hamilton Holt (ed.), *Undistinguished Americans*, James Pott & Co., 1906.

Two years later

I and Francesco are to be American in three years. The court gave us papers and said we must wait and we must be able to read some things and tell who the ruler of the country is.

There are plenty of rich Italians here; the richest ones go away from the other Italians and live with the Americans. Francesco and I have a room to ourselves and some people call us 'swells'. Francesco bought a gold watch with a gold chain.

C Welcome to all!

A view of immigration by Joseph Keppler, himself an immigrant. This cartoon appeared in Puck in 1880.

Questions

1 What did Louis Adamic mean by saying he thought of America as the 'Golden Country'?

2 Compare Source 10A with Louis Adamic's boyhood impressions of America. What disappointments might he have had in the USA?

3 Can you think of reasons why returned emigrants might exaggerate in their stories?

4 What did the Americanec in Source A mean when he spoke of the difference between a 'subject' and a 'citizen'? How does this idea relate to Sources B and C?

5 What would Rocco Corresca have been able to do with $200?

6 What is the cartoonist saying about immigrants' reasons for leaving their homeland?

7 What advantages does he suggest the USA can offer them?

12 Ludlow, 1914

*Most American employers were ruthless in dealing with workers' organisations.
During strikes they often brought in workers from another district to act as strike
breakers. In some cases employers even used armed men to prevent workers setting up
unions. This happened in the strike at Ludlow in the Colorado mining fields in
1913–14.*

*The United Mine Workers' Union called a strike on 25 September 1913, after
the owners refused to talk about safety regulations. The employers then drove between eight and ten thousand miners and their families from their company-owned
homes. In reply the Union set up a 'colony' of tents near the mine works. The
Company hired a private army under Lieutenant Linderfelt to break the strike.
Militiamen of the Colorado State Guard were also used against the strikers.*

*Source A describes an attack on the strikers' tents. It is taken from a Report
written in 1915 for the US Commission on Industrial Relations.*

A Report on the Ludlow Strike

Although twelve hundred men, women and children remained at the
Ludlow Tent Colony and Lieutenant Linderfelt's guards consisted of
not more than thirty five men, they were equipped with machine guns
and repeating rifles. Linderfelt believed the strikers to be unarmed.

On April 20th Linderfelt's men destroyed the Ludlow colony, killing
five men and one boy and firing the tents with a torch.

Eleven children and two women who had taken refuge were burned
to death or suffocated after the tents had been fired. During the fire,
Linderfelt's men looted the tents of everything that appealed to their
fancy.

Three of the strikers killed at Ludlow were shot while under the
guard of Linderfelt's men. They included Louis Tikas, a leader of the
Greek strikers, a man of high intelligence, who had done his utmost to
maintain peace. Tikas was first seriously wounded by a blow on the
head from the stock of a rifle in the hands of Lieutenant Linderfelt and
then shot three times in the back by militiamen and mine guards.

Two days after the Ludlow tragedy the responsible leaders of organized labor in Colorado telegraphed to President Wilson notifying
him that they had sent an appeal to every labor organization in Colorado urging them to gather arms and to organize themselves into
companies.

By Wednesday, April 22nd the miners over a wide area attacked
mine after mine, driving off or killing the guards and setting fire to the
buildings. These mines were manned by superintendents, foremen,
mine guards and strikebreakers.

Later a party of about 200 armed strikers, mostly Greeks, poured a
deadly fire into the Forbes camp. Nine mine guards and strikebreakers
were shot to death and one striker was killed.

From R. Hofstadter and
M. Wallace, *American
Violence: A Documentary
History*, Alfred A. Knopf
Inc., 1960.

B Before Linderfelt's attack *A photograph of the miners' tents before the attack.*

C After Linderfelt's attack *Red Cross workers searching the ruins of the tent colony.*

Questions

1 In what way do the first four paragraphs of the Report suggest that Linderfelt's attack on the tents was a deliberate attempt to terrorise the strikers?

2 Why do you think the Colorado labour leaders told the President of their plans to arm the workers?

3 Linderfelt's men were a 'private army'. What sort of men might join such a force? What justification would the owners give for hiring them?

4 The strike ended in December 1914. In what ways might coal owners later get their revenge on the strike leaders?

5 What do the two photographs tell you about events at Ludlow in 1913–14? Do they confirm any parts of the Report?

Part 4

★★★★★★★★★★★★★★★★★★★★★★★★★★★★

The emergence of the USA as a world power

13 The 'Lusitania' affair

On 7 May 1915 the British Cunard liner, Lusitania, *travelling from New York, was torpedoed by a German U-boat near the south coast of Ireland. Nearly 1,200 passengers and crew were lost including 128 American citizens. In the United States, anti-German feeling swept the country. Few knew that the* Lusitania *was carrying cases of ammunition for the British army. President Wilson sent strong messages to the German government who agreed to limit their U-boat campaign. Some American politicians believed that Wilson was leaning too much towards the Allies (Britain and France). One was William Jennings Bryan, the Secretary of State – or foreign affairs minister. He resigned over this disagreement.*

In these extracts the writer, E. R. Ellis, uses contemporay reports to build his own reconstruction of the events of May 1915.

A Departure of the *Lusitania*, 1 May 1915

There was something different about this departure. Morning editions of New York papers had published, next to a paid Cunard schedule, this strange notice:

> TRAVELERS intending to embark on the Atlantic voyage are reminded that a state of war exists between Germany and her allies and Great Britain and her allies; that the zone of war includes the water adjacent to the British Isles; that, in accordance with formal notice given by the Imperial German Government, vessels flying the flag of Great Britain, or any of her allies, are liable to destruction in those waters. . . .
>
> IMPERIAL GERMAN EMBASSY

. . . One of the reporters now aboard the Lusitania showed the embassy's advertisement to the ship's senior third officer, John Lewis, and asked to see the captain. Lewis refused. Instead, he had someone telephone Charles Sumner, the New York general manager of the Cunard line, asking him to come to the pier and speak to the press.

Some Lusitania passengers had read the notice and reacted in terms of their personalities – they winced or shuddered or laughed. William H. Brown of Buffalo, New York, did not laugh; the previous night he

From E. R. Ellis, *Echoes of a Distant Thunder*, Coward, McCann & Geoghegan Inc., 1975.

had dreamed the Lusitania was torpedoed and he was lost at sea. . . .
At the last minute the Reverend W. M. Warlow of Bennington, Vermont, became so frightened he cancelled his reservation and booked himself instead on the 'New York' of the American line. . . .

The Cunard representative, Charles Sumner, came aboard. . . . When asked by the press what he thought about the warning from the Germany embassy, he gestured at the passengers boarding the great liner and laughed. 'You can see how it has affected the public.' Had anyone cancelled his reservation? No, Sumner replied, not a single one.

B Sinking of the *Lusitania*, 7 May 1915

On this sunny day the time was now 2:09 p.m.

Schwieger [the U-boat skipper] cried, 'Fire!' . . . The Lusitania sinks in eighteen minutes. . . .

President Wilson had finished lunch in the White House and was about to leave for a golf course when a clerk handed him a bulletin about the Lusitania . . . His eyes were sad. Rescue ships were bringing survivors to Queenstown, Ireland. . . . Aware that Americans had been killed by Germans, conscious that this would imperil his neutrality policy, facing his most severe test since taking office, Wilson could hardly bear the news. In the evening he surprised his secret service guard by leaving the White House, walking out into the night and a light rainfall. . . .

Only a few blocks away, Bryan mused aloud to his wife, 'I wonder if that ship carried munitions of war? If she did carry them, it puts a different face on the whole matter! England has been using our citizens to protect her ammunition. . . .'

[The *Lusitania* carried 4,200 cases of ammunition.]

From E. R. Ellis, Echoes of a Distant Thunder, Coward, McCann & Geoghegan Inc., 1975.

Questions

1 Why did the Germany embassy publish the newspaper notice?

2 Can you explain why Sumner claimed that no one had cancelled their reservation?

3 What questions would you have asked Mr Sumner if you had been a reporter on sailing day?

4 Why should the sinking of the *Lusitania* 'imperil' Wilson's 'neutrality policy'?

5 Draw posters showing the sinking of the *Lusitania* from
(a) a German viewpoint and
(b) a pro-war American viewpoint.

6 This account is a reconstruction written sixty years after the events took place. Can you see any places where the writer may have used mostly his imagination?

14 The United States enters the world war

After the sinking of the Lusitania *in 1915 relations between Germany and the USA grew steadily worse. In the spring of 1917 they broke down altogether. The German military leaders believed that their only chance of victory lay in sinking all ships which carried supplies to Britain and France, even if this meant war with the USA. On 31 January they announced that unrestricted submarine warfare against merchant ships would begin the next day. On 1 March the Americans discovered that the German government had told its ambassador in Mexico to make an alliance with that country. Mexico was told that this could be their chance to take back Texas, Arizona and New Mexico which had all been seized by the USA in the nineteenth century. On 12 and 19 March four unarmed American merchant ships were sunk without warning, by German U-boats.*

On 2 April President Wilson went to Congress to make this speech, asking them to declare war on Germany. Four days later they agreed.

A Wilson's message to Congress, April 1917

I have called the Congress into extraordinary session because there are very serious choices of policy to be made immediately, which it was neither right nor constitutionally permissible that I should assume the responsibility of making.

On the third of February last I officially laid before you the announcement of the Imperial German Government that on and after the first day of February it was its purpose to put aside all restraints of law and humanity and use its submarines to sink every vessel that sought to approach either the ports of Great Britain and Ireland or the western coasts of Europe or any of the ports controlled by the enemies of Germany within the Mediterranean.

It is a war against all nations. American ships have been sunk, American lives taken, but the ships and people of other neutral and friendly nations have been sunk and overwhelmed in the waters in the same way. There has been no discrimination. The challenge is to all mankind. Each nation must decide for itself how it will meet it. We must put excited feeling away. Our motive will not be revenge or the victorious assertion of the physical might of the nation, but only the vindication of right, of human right, of which we are only a single champion . . .

In unhesitating obedience to what I deem my constitutional duty, I advise Congress declare the recent course of the Imperial German Government to be in fact nothing less than war against the government and people of the United States; that it formally accept the status of belligerent; and that it take immediate steps not only to put the country into a more thorough state of defense but also to exert all its power and employ all its resources to bring the government of the German Empire to terms and end the war . . .

Woodrow Wilson's war message delivered to the Senate, 65th Congress, 1st Session, 1917.

We have no quarrel with the German people. We have no feeling towards them but one of sympathy and friendship. It was not upon their impulse that their government acted in entering this war. It was not with their previous knowledge or approval.

There are, it may be, many months of fiery trial and sacrifice ahead of us. It is a fearful thing to lead this great peaceful people into war, into the most terrible and disastrous of all wars. But the right is more precious than peace, and we shall fight for the things which we have always carried nearest to our hearts – for democracy, for the right of those who submit to authority to have a voice in their own governments, for the rights and liberties of small nations, for a universal dominion of right by such a concert of free peoples as shall bring peace and safety to all nations and make the world itself at last free.

Questions

1 What two reasons does Wilson give for not declaring war himself?

2 What reason does he give for the USA taking 'the status of a belligerent'?

3 Was it reasonable to say that the war would not be against the German people? Give reasons for your answer.

4 What war aims does Wilson set out at the end of the speech? In what ways are they the same as the ideas in his 'Fourteen Points' of January 1918?

5 Write two letters, dated April 1917, in which two Americans argue for and against war with Germany.

15 A prisoner of war remembers

In February 1917 the Germans opened unrestricted submarine warfare on American and other neutral ships. In April the USA replied by declaring war on Germany and soon the first American troops were fighting with the Allies. By 1918 the German armies, commanded by Field Marshal von Hindenburg, were being ground into defeat. The German people were becoming weary of the war and the shortages of food.

Frank Savicki had emigrated to the USA from Poland before he joined the American army. Towards the end of the war he was captured by the Germans and sent to Laon prisoner-of-war camp in eastern France, which was then still occupied by Germany. From there he was sent to another camp in Germany itself where he worked on a farm. Later, he escaped and was the first American prisoner to get out of Germany.

Frank Savicki's experiences were published in the United States soldiers' magazine, Stars and Stripes, *in 1918.*

A Memories of Frank Savicki

In France

In the morning and at night, marching to and from work, we used to try to gather grass along the roadside. We would take this back to camp with us and make soup of it. The French prisoners cooked it in the prison yard, flavoring it liberally with salt. Salt is the only thing in Germany, so far as I know, of which they have plenty.

Living conditions were terrible, there were no beds in the barracks and none of us had blankets. We slept on the bare floor. No one had a change of clothes and there was no means of washing those we had. In all the month and a half I was at Laon I did not have my clothes off. Everybody was covered with lice.

In Germany

German soldiers on the front line eat fairly well. They all have bread, meat once a day, marmalade, coffee substitute and tobacco made of leaves.

The soldiers 20 or 30 miles [30 or 50 kilometres] behind the front line, however, do not get the same ration. They have meat only two or three times a week and they exist mainly on war bread and vegetables. In Germany itself there is little food of any kind. The farmer, where I worked, had chickens and cows but only rarely did they have milk and eggs themselves and never did they give me more than a boiled potato in hot water.

After I had been on the farm a week the farmer's son arrived from the front for a furlough. As soon as he arrived he took off his uniform and all his equipment and sent it back to the front.

America, the son told me, had turned the scales of war, and Germany

From Herbert Mitgang (ed.), *Civilian under Arms*, Pennington Press, 1959.

had no hope. He complained of shortage of everything at the front. He believed that the United States was fighting for the money she would make out of it and that the American soldiers were fighting because they were so highly paid. I heard many Germans condemning Hindenburg. Some of them said that if he were dead the war would be over and everything would be all right.

B Conscription

Attention!

ALL MALES between the ages of 21 and 30 years, both inclusive, must personally appear at the polling place in the Election District in which they reside, on

TUESDAY, JUNE 5th, 1917

between the hours of 7 A.M. and 9 P. M. and

Register

in accordance with the President's Proclamation.

Any male person, between these ages, who fails to register on June 5th, 1917, will be subject to imprisonment in jail or other penal institution for a term of one year.

NO EXCUSE FOR FAILURE TO REGISTER WILL BE ACCEPTED

NON-RESIDENTS must apply personally for registration, at the office of the County Clerk, at Kingston, N. Y., AT ONCE, in order that their registration cards may be in the hands of the Registration Board of their home district before June 5, 1917

Employers of males between these ages are earnestly requested to assist in the enforcement of the President's Proclamation.

Signed,

BOARD OF REGISTRATION
of Ulster County
E. T. SHULTIS, Sheriff
C. K. LOUGHRAN, County Clerk
Dr. FRANK JOHNSTON, Medical Officer

Congress passed a law for conscription in May 1917. A few days later notices such as this appeared throughout the USA.

Questions

1 What examples of German food shortages can you find in the passage?

2 Why would even a farmer's family be short of food?

3 What is meant by 'furlough'? Why did the German farmer's son send his equipment back to the battle front?

4 In what way could the USA be said to have 'turned the scales of war'?

5 What does Source B tell you about one of the two ways in which soldiers joined the army? What was the other way?

6 Why do you think the registration age was twenty-one in the USA and much lower in other countries fighting the war?

16 Woodrow Wilson and the League of Nations

Woodrow Wilson was the son of a Presbyterian Minister who spent many years as a university lecturer. He first entered politics to become governor of New Jersey and was elected President, as a Democrat, in 1912. In 1917 he led the United States into war against Germany and this made him powerful enough to take a leading part in the peace conference at Versailles in 1919. He persuaded Britain, France and Italy to agree to a League of Nations but many Americans feared that this would mean that their country would be forever involved in European quarrels.

In September 1919 Wilson made an exhausting journey westwards across the USA to try and win public support for the Covenant which set out the aims of the League of Nations. Leading figures in the Republican Party such as Henry Cabot Lodge were already saying that the Senate should refuse to sign the Covenant.

Starting in Ohio, Wilson made thirty-seven speeches in twenty-two days. The strain of this tour on top of seven years as President made him too ill to carry on with active politics between the end of September 1919 and April 1920. In that time his secretary, Joseph Tumulty, and his wife did their best to conceal how ill he was and would not let even political supporters talk to him. Without his leadership the Senate voted, in November 1919 and March 1920, to refuse the United States' agreement to the Treaty of Versailles and the Covenant of the League. The story is told by G. S. Viereck, a journalist who was close to Wilson at the time.

A Woodrow Wilson in decline

On September 3rd the battered, broken, one-eyed Covenanter sets forth upon his crusade. He makes a notable speech in Columbus, Ohio ....

In Pueblo, on September 25, no longer master of his emotions, Woodrow Wilson bursts into tears when he addresses the crowd. His headaches rob him of sleep. When he sleeps, saliva drops from the corner of his mouth. Fever assails his body. Catastrophe is at hand.

At four o'clock in the morning, on September 26, Grayson knocks at Tumulty's compartment. 'The President is seriously ill. I greatly fear that the trip may end fatally if he attempts to go on.'

When Tumulty arrives at the President's drawing-room, he finds him fully dressed and seated in his chair. Speech no longer flows freely. His tongue stumbles. His lips refuse to articulate. His face is ghostly pale, one side of it seems to have fallen, like a ruined house. Tears stream down the President's cheek. ...

The sick man pleads with his doctor and his secretary. 'Don't you see that if you cancel this trip, Senator Lodge and his friends will say that I am a quitter, and that the Western trip was a failure, and the Treaty will be lost! ...'

Wilson is unable to persuade Tumulty. His left arm and leg no longer function.

From G. S. Viereck, *The Strangest Friendship in History*, Duckworth, 1933.

The train slides into a siding near Wichita, Kansas ... Mrs. Wilson, now thoroughly alarmed, takes command of the situation. ... A sign from her ends the sad crusade ... the train turns homeward. Blinds down, it swiftly heads to Washington. ...

On November 18, a curious dramatic situation occurs. The President is permitted, for the second time since he is stricken, to sun himself on the south lawn of the White House. From the windows of the Cabinet Room, the members of the Cabinet, while in session, would see the President in his wheel chair. They could see him but could not reach or communicate with him. Senator Gilbert M. Hitchcock is equally unlucky. He leads the fight for the Treaty that is most dear to Wilson's heart, but the sick room is locked against him. ...

Questions

1 What impression of Woodrow Wilson do you get from this account?

2 What strains might have led to his illness?

3 How would his illness affect the efforts of Senators such as Gilbert Hitchcock?

4 Does this passage give any hints that the League Covenant might still not have been signed even if Wilson had been active?

Part 5
★★★★★★★★★★★★★★★★★★★★★★★★★
Boom and bust

17 Izzy and prohibition

The Volstead Act, which was passed in 1920, aimed to stop Americans from making, selling and drinking alcohol. Government 'prohibition' agents had the job of tracking down illegal bars or 'speakeasies'.

Izzy Einstein, a short, chubby man, was a very famous prohibition agent – so famous that his portrait hung in many illegal bars! With his partner, Moe Smith, Izzy made over 4,000 arrests and confiscated drinks worth millions of dollars. He was successful in collecting the evidence needed to make convictions in court and used simple disguises to get past the doorkeepers of speakeasies.

A journalist, Herbert Asbury, used stories about Izzy in New York newspapers of the time to give him the material for this description of his work.

A Izzy Einstein

Izzy's first assignment was to clean up a place in Brooklyn which the enforcement authorities shrewdly suspected housed a 'speakeasy', since drunken men had been seen staggering from the building, and the air for half a block around was full with the fumes of beer and whisky. Several agents had snooped and slunk around the house, but none had been able to get inside. Izzy knew nothing of detective procedures; he simply walked up to the joint and knocked on the door. A peephole was opened and a hoarse voice demanded to know who was there.

'Izzy Einstein,' said Izzy. 'I want a drink'. 'Oh yeah? Who sent you here, bud? What's your business?'

'My boss sent me,' Izzy explained. 'I'm a prohibition agent. I just got appointed.'

The door swung open and the doorman slapped Izzy jovially on the back.

'Ho! Ho!' he cried. 'Come right in, bud. That's the best gag I've heard yet.'

Izzy stepped into a room where half a dozen men were drinking at a small make-shift bar.

'Hey, boss!' the doorman yelled. 'Here's a prohibition agent wants a drink! You got a badge too bud?'

'Sure I have,' said Izzy, and produced it.

'Well I'm damned,' said the man behind the bar. 'Looks just like the real thing.'

From I. Leighton (ed.), *The Aspirin Age 1919–41*, Simon & Schuster, 1949.

He poured a slug of whisky, and Izzy downed it. That was a mistake for when the time came to 'make the pinch' Izzy had no evidence. He tried to grab the bottle, but the bartender ran out of the back door with it.

'I learned right there,' said Izzy, 'that a slug of hooch [spirits] in an agent's belly might feel good, but it ain't evidence.'

So when he went home that night he rigged up an evidence collector. He put a small funnel in the upper left hand pocket of his vest [waistcoat] and connected it, by means of a rubber tube, with a flat bottle concealed in the lining of the garment. Thereafter, when a drink was served to him, Izzy took a small sip, then poured the remainder into the funnel while the bartender was making change [at the till]. There was always enough for analysis and to offer in evidence.

'I'd have died if it hadn't been for that little funnel and the bottle' said Izzy. 'Most of the stuff I got in those places was terrible.'

B   Illicit stills seized in the USA

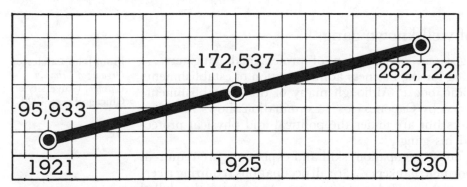

95,933   172,537   282,122

1921   1925   1930

Questions

1 What was a speakeasy? How do you think it got its name?

2 Most prohibition agents were not so good at their jobs as Izzy was. Why do you think Izzy was so successful?

3 Where do you think people made drink to avoid getting caught? Why do you think it was so terrible?

4 Imagine you owned some illegal bars. Design a notice for your bartenders to advise them on how to keep agents out.

5 Look carefully at the graph.
   (a) What was the increase in the number of stills seized between 1921 and 1930?
   (b) What other figures would you need to prove whether or not this increase was due to the success of the prohibition agents?

18 The age of the gangsters

In Chicago, gangsters such as Dion O'Bannion and Al Capone made huge for-
tunes from illegal drink. By 1927 Capone's crime business had earned him $60
million from selling alcohol and $45 million from gambling clubs and other rackets.

Both gang leaders employed specialist crooks who worked in the speakeasies and
the gambling clubs. Among them were 'ropers' to attract customers, 'friskers' who
searched for weapons and 'bankers' who worked at the gambling tables. To protect
their businesses the gang bosses spent millions of dollars on paying their gunmen
and in bribing policemen and politicians. Much money was spent on fixing elec-
tions so that men in the gangsters' pay were chosen for the Chicago city council.

These two passages are taken from a study of criminal organisations by John
Landesco. The study was part of a massive Illinois State Crime Survey, and was
published in 1929.

In the first extract Landesco describes the two gangs and how O'Bannion saw to
it that his man won the election in the city's river ward (the local electoral district).
In the second he describes the party, or 'wake', after O'Bannion's funeral,
which was attended by many leading figures in Chicago.

A Organisation of well-known gangs

The Capone Gang is an organization of professional gangsters. . . .
The gang was formed for the business administration of establishments
of vice, gambling and booze. Although many of these establishments
are reported as owned by Capone, closer examination shows that they
have separate owners but are under the political and physical protec-
tion of Capone and his gang.

In the gambling house occupation, skill and experience are required.
Ropers, friskers, doormen, bankers . . . are all occupations requiring a cer-
tain apprenticeship and knowledge of customer. Apart from the skilled
jobs, the syndicate has always had its standing army of gunmen
which could be increased in time of trouble and reduced to a few body-
guards in time of peace. In the Capone 'mob' these were recruited from
known, reliable trigger men from all over the city and outside, but the
dominant element was always Italian.

The O'Bannion gang is similar to the Capone gang in that it is a
union of adults for 'business' purposes, each having served his earlier
apprenticeship and having established his reputation in his own
neighbourhood.

Dion O'Bannion toured the river ward in his own peculiar fashion.
After the kidnappings, sluggings and threats of death and after the
votes had been counted, there was reason for rejoicing in the O'Bannion headquarters. Crowe [O'Bannion's candidate] had won by a large
margin. To get everybody in a proper frame of mind to obey election
day orders, O'Bannion wandered into saloons and would casually cut
loose with a couple of guns. . . .

From John Landesco,
Organized Crime in
Chicago, University of
Chicago Press, 1929.

B O'Bannion's funeral and wake

Flowers came to the chapel in truck loads. There was a huge wreath from the Teamsters' Union and a basket of roses bore the card of Al (Scarface) Capone.

Alderman Crowe was at the wake so were Judges Burke, La Buy, Schulman, O'Connell and Borrelli of the Municipal Court. O'Bannion lay in state in the Chapel of the Undertaking Rooms at 708 North Wells Street in a ten thousand dollar casket [coffin]. It was the 'best that money could buy'.

Thousands and thousands lined sidewalks [payements], stood on fire escapes and on roofs, as the twenty-four automobiles full of flowers, the one hundred twenty-two funeral cars, the scores of private cars and the hearse carrying the ten thousand dollar silver and bronze casket rolled slowly by.

From John Landesco, *Organized Crime in Chicago*, University of Chicago Press, 1929.

Questions

1 In your own words describe how the gangs were made up. Why are the words 'syndicate' and 'union' used to describe them?

2 What sort of organisation was the Capone gang and why was it formed?

3 What was a 'trigger man'? What kind of people might have taken up such 'work'?

4 Describe how O'Bannion fixed the election in the river ward.

5 Name three important people who attended O'Bannion's funeral. What favours might they have done for O'Bannion?

6 Why do you think so many people were attracted to a gangster's funeral?

7 Imagine you are either a shopkeeper or a clerk in the Chicago housing department. Write a letter to a friend explaining how the gangs interfere in your work.

19 Just a family gathering?

The Ku Klux Klan had almost faded away after its anti-black violence described in Source 1. It revived again after World War One and grew rapidly in numbers. By 1925 the Klan had 5 million members. This new Klan turned its hatred against anyone considered to be un-American, including blacks, Catholics, Jews and recent immigrants. It began to use modern methods and an army of salesmen to spread its message.

In this passage written in the 1930s, Robert Coughlan, who later became a writer for Life *magazine, recalls his experiences as a young Catholic boy. He remembers going to a huge rally of 200,000 Klansmen in Indiana State. The star guest was the leader of the Indiana Klan, David Stephenson, who begins his visit with the Klan code words of greeting.*

A The Ku Klux Klan

On a hot July day in Kokomo Central Indiana a great crowd of oddly dressed people clustered around an open meadow. Their faces, framed in white hoods, were expectant, and their eyes searched the bright sky. Suddenly they began to cheer. They had seen it – a speck that grew into an aeroplane.

A bulky man in robe and hood of purple silk climbed down to the ground and a new surge of applause filled the country air. A small delegation of dignitaries filed out towards the plane.

The man in purple stepped forward.

'Kigy,' he said.

'Itsub,' they replied solemnly.

The man in purple walked forward to the rostrum and held up his right hand to hush the excited crowd.

'My worthy subjects, citizens of the Invisible Empire, Klansmen all, greetings!'

He urged his audience to fight for 'one hundred per cent Americanism' and to stop 'foreign elements' that he said were trying to control the country. As he finished and stepped back, a coin came spinning through the air. Soon people were throwing rings, money, watch charms, anything bright and valuable...

My father suggested that we drive out to see what was happening. We saw white-sheeted Klansmen everywhere, walking about with their hoods thrown back, eating in restaurants. The road was a creeping mass of cars. They were draped with flags and bunting and some carried home-made signs with Klan slogans as 'America for the Americans' or 'The Pope will sit in the White House when Hell freezes over...'

The rest of the day, after Stephenson's speech, was given over to sports, band concerts and general holiday frolic. That night there was a parade down Main Street in Kokomo. There were thirty bands; but as

From I. Leighton (ed.), *The Aspirin Age 1919–41*, Simon & Schuster, 1949.

usual in Klan parades there was no music, only the sound of drums. They rolled the slow, heavy tempo of the march to a low meadow where the Klan had put up a twenty-five foot 'fiery cross'. Many of the marchers carried flaming torches. Flag bearers usually carried two Klan flags flanking an American flag, and the word would ripple down the rows of spectators lining the kerbs, 'Here comes the flag!' and 'Hats off for the flag!' Near the place where I was standing with my parents one man was slow with his hat and had it knocked off his head. He started to protest, thought better of it, and held his hat in his hand during the rest of the parade.

Questions

1 What would you have found exciting about the Klan rally? What would you have found frightening or disturbing?

2 Why do you think the Coughlan family went to watch the Klan, their enemies?

3 Why did Klansmen use coded pass words and strange titles. Why were only drums played?

4 What evidence is there in the passage that the Klan were against Roman Catholics?

5 Compare this passage with Source 2 on page 4. In what ways had the Klan changed between the 1860s and 1920s? What do you think were the reasons for the revival of the Klan in the 1920s?

6 Stephenson thought only white, Anglo-Saxon Protestants (WASPs) were one hundred per cent Americans worthy of full rights. What arguments would you use against his definition?

20 Bonus marchers

After 1929 unemployment rocketed in the United States. Millions could not afford to pay their rent or to buy food and had to seek help from public charity. In 1932, 25,000 World War One veterans and other unemployed people marched on foot or took free rides to Washington DC, the capital. They went to demand that the government gave them part payment of the bonuses they had earned as soldiers in the war. President Hoover, however, refused their demand.

Jim Sheridan was not a veteran, but he joined the band of marchers which went from Chicago. Here he describes how the marchers camped in a main street or in 'Hoovervilles' which was the name given by the unemployed to districts of shanty houses. Police refused to turn the marchers out of the city but this was done by regular army troops led by General Douglas MacArthur. In the late 1960s Jim Sheridan told his story to a social historian, Studs Terkel, who included it in his book about the depression.

A Jim Sheridan's story

We went down to the railyards and grabbed a freight train, some of the fellas had come with their families. Of course, the railroad companies didn't know this, but these conductors, out of their sympathy would put two or three empty boxcars in the train, so these bonus marchers could crawl into them and ride comfortable into Washington. . . .

When we got to Washington, there was quite a few ex-servicemen there before us. There was no arrangements for housing. Most of the men that had wives and children were living in Hooverville. They had set up housing made of cardboard and of all kinds. I don't know how they managed to get their food. Most other contingents were along Pennsylvania Avenue [the road to the White House].

They had come to petition President Hoover, to give them the bonus before it was due. And Hoover refused this.

The question was now: How were they going to get them out of Washington? They were ordered out four or five times and they refused. The police chief was called to send them out but he refused. I also heard that the marine commander also refused. Finally the one they did get to shove these bedraggled ex-servicemen out of Washington was none other than the great MacArthur. He was riding a white horse. Behind him were tanks, troops of the regular army.

When these ex-soldiers wouldn't move, they'd poke them with their bayonets and hit them on the head with the butt of a rifle. They had a hell of a time getting them out of the buildings they were in.

As night fell they crossed the Potomac [river]. They were given orders to get out of Anacostia Flats [marshes] and they refused.

The soldiers set those shanties on fire. They were practically smoked out.

And so the bonus marchers straggled back to the various places they came from. And without their bonus.

From Studs Terkel, *Hard Times*, Allen Lane, 1970.

B The marchers are driven out of Washington, 1932

Questions

1 Why did the bonus marchers demand their bonuses early?

2 What clues are there in the extract to suggest that many people were sympathetic to the bonus marchers?

3 Why do you think the police force refused to turn the bonus marchers out?

4 Why did the unemployed name their shanty town after the President?

5 Imagine you were one of the soldiers. Write a letter describing how you had treated the marchers under your officer's orders and how you felt about what you had done.

6 Does the photograph give the same impressions of the soldiers' treatment of the bonus marchers as Sheridan's account? In what ways are the two pieces of evidence different?

7 How would you check whether Sheridan's memory could be relied upon? What other types of evidence would you consult?

21 'Brother, Can You Spare A Dime?'

In the winter of 1932–33 nearly a quarter of all the USA's workers were unemployed. With no chance of work and all their savings gone, many sold apples on the pavements and slept on park benches or in shacks or shanties.

Some begged, hoping for ten cents, a dime, from passers-by. Thousands queued for hours in 'bread lines' for a free handout of bread and soup from a private charity. One of the biggest food charities in New York City was run by the millionaire newspaper owner, William Randolph Hearst.

'Yip' Harburg, a famous song writer of the time, saw the desperate position of the unemployed. Here he recalls the 'depression' years and tells Studs Terkel, a social historian writing in the 1960s, how he got the ideas for the most famous song of the early 1930s. At the time the Republican President Hoover was facing Roosevelt, the Democrat Party Candidate, in a presidential election campaign.

A Yip Harburg

I was walking along the street at the time, and you'd see the bread lines. The biggest one in New York City was owned by William Randolph Hearst. He had a big truck with several people on it, and big cauldrons of hot soup, bread.

There was a sketch in one of the first shows I did, 'Americana'. This was 1930. In the sketch, Mrs. Ogden Reid, owner of the 'Herald Tribune' newspaper was very jealous of Hearst's beautiful bread line. It was bigger than her bread line. It was a satirical, lively show. We needed a song for it.

On stage we had men in old soldiers' uniform, dilapidated, waiting around. And then into the song. We had to have a title . . . my wife is sick, I've got six children. The Crash* put me out of business, hand me a dime.

The prevailing greeting at that time, on every street corner you passed, by some poor guy coming up, was: 'Can you spare a dime?' Or: 'Can you spare something for a cup of coffee?' . . . 'Brother, Can You Spare a Dime?' finally hit on every street.

This is the man who says: 'I built the railroads, I built that tower. I fought your wars. Why the hell should I be standing in line now? What happened to all this wealth I created?' The song makes him a dignified human, asking questions – a bit outraged too, as he should be.

Everybody picked the song up in '30 and '31. Bands were playing it and records were made. When Roosevelt was a candidate for President the Republicans got pretty worried about it. In some cases they tried to ban it from the radio. But it was too late. The song had already done its damage.

From Studs Terkel, *Hard Times*, Allen Lane, 1970.

*Wall Street Crash, 1929. Thousands lost money as the price of stocks and shares tumbled

B Brother, Can You Spare a Dime?

They used to tell me I was building a dream
with peace and glory ahead
why should I be standing in line
just waiting for bread?

Once I built a railroad, made it run
made it race against time
once I built a railroad, now it's done—
Brother can you spare a dime?

Once w' Khaki suits, gee we looked swell,
full of that Yankee Doodle de dum
Half a million boots went slogging thro' hell,
I was the kid with the drum.

Say, don't you remember, they called me Al
Gee, it was Al all the time
Say, don't you remember
I'm your Pal! Buddy
Can you spare a dime?

From E. Y. Harburg, 'Brother Can You Spare A Dime?', Harms Inc., 1932.

Questions

1 What was a bread line? Why are there no bread lines today when people are out of work?

2 Explain what sort of scene, or sketch, Yip Harburg was writing this song for.

3 Where did Yip Harburg get the idea for his title from?

4 What was the point of the sketch Yip Harburg describes in the first paragraph?

5 In your own words explain what the song is saying and why its message is so sharp.

6 Why would the Republican Party and President Hoover have been worried by the song's popularity in 1930–31?

7 Write down some lines from a modern song which is popular because it draws attention to a social problem.

Part 6

★★★★★★★★★★★★★★★★★★★★★★★★★★★★★
Roosevelt and the New Deal

22 Looking for work

During the 1930s there was a great deal of migration in the United States. Poor farmers left the parched, dried up lands of the Mid-West and hundreds of thousands of blacks were leaving the cotton plantations and farms of the South. They headed north to look for jobs in cities like Chicago. Many people became 'hobos', or travellers, stealing a ride on freight trains as they roamed the United States looking for work.

The following extract tells of some of the experiences of a black hobo, Louis Banks. Banks eventually found work with the Works Progress Administration (WPA), a huge government public works scheme which put millions of unemployed Americans back to work. When World War Two came, he joined the United States Army.

In the late 1960s Studs Terkel, a social historian, interviewed Banks about his experiences. The extract below was part of the interview.

A Louis Banks, a black hobo

1929 was pretty hard. I hoboed. I begged for a nickel to get something to eat. They didn't hire me because I didn't belong to the right kind of race. Another time I went into Saginaw – it was two white fellas and myself. The fella there hired the two men and didn't hire me. I was back out on the streets. That hurt me pretty bad, the race apart.

When I was hoboing, I would lay on the side of the tracks and wait until I could see a train comin'. I would always carry a bottle of water in my pocket and a piece of tape or rag to keep it from bustin' and put a piece of bread in my pocket, so I wouldn't starve on the way. . . .

Black and white, it didn't make any difference who you were, 'cause everybody was poor. We used to take a big pot and cook food, cabbage, meat and beans all together. We all set together, made a tent. Twenty-five or thirty would be out on the side of the rail, white or colored. They didn't have no mothers or sisters, they didn't have no home, they were dirty. They didn't have no food, they didn't have anything.

Sometimes we sent one hobo to walk, to see if there were any jobs open. He'd come back and say, 'Detroit, no job'. He'd say 'They're hiring in New York City'. So we went to New York City. Sometimes ten or fifteen of us would be on the train. And I'd hear one of 'em holler. He'd fall off. He'd get killed. He was trying to get off the train.

From Studs Terkel, *Hard Times*, Allen Lane, 1970.

I knocked on people's doors. They'd say 'what do you want?' 'I'll call the police.' And they'd put you in jail for vagrancy. They'd make you milk cows thirty or ninety days. Up in Wisconsin, they'd do the same thing. Alabama they'd do the same thing. California, anywhere you'd go. Always in jail, and I never did nothin'.

I had fifteen or twenty jobs from six o'clock in the morning till seven o'clock at night. I was fixin' the meat, cookin', washing the dishes and cleanin' up. Just like you threw the ball at one end and run down and catch it on the other. You're Jack of all trades. White chefs were getting forty dollars a week but I was getting 21 for doin' what they were doin' and everthin' else. The poor people had it rough.

Worked on the W.P.A. and earn 27 dollars 50 cents. We just dig a ditch and cover it back up. You thought you was rich. You could buy a suit of clothes.

When the war came, I was so glad when I got in the army. I knew I was safe. I had money comin'. I had food comin' and I had a lot of gang around me. I knew on the streets or hoboing, I might be killed any time.

Questions

1 What would be the high and low moments in the life of a hobo?

2 What image does Louis Banks use to describe the endless tasks of his kitchen job?

3 What comments does Banks make about when black hobos did and did not experience racial prejudice?

4 Why did many states imprison homeless vagrants in the 1930s?

5 Why did Banks feel there was less risk of being killed in the army than in hoboing?

23 The dust bowl

A disastrously dry summer and high winds in 1934 turned large areas of the Mid-West into a huge dust bowl. Farmers who owned or rented land in Arkansas, Oklahoma and surrounding states now had land which produced nothing. The numbers of farmers and tenants shrank as banks and large landowners took over their farms when they could no longer pay their mortgages or rents.

Many of the people piled their belongings on to farm trucks and drove West in search of the 'promised land' – California.

John Steinbeck, in a famous novel, The Grapes of Wrath, *described this huge movement of families. The book is based partly on his own experiences in the Mid-West during the 1930s. Here Steinbeck is writing about the dust bowl in Oklahoma where in places the soil was grey and in others the colour of red clay.*

A John Steinbeck

The sun flared down on the growing corn day after day until a line of brown spread along the edge of each green bayonet. The clouds appeared, and went away, and in a while they did not try any more ... The surface of the earth crusted, a thin hard crust, and as the sky became pale, so the earth became pale, pink in the red country, and white in the grey country ...

In the roads where the teams moved, where the wheels milled the ground and the hooves of the horses beat the ground, the dirt crust broke and the dust formed. Every moving thing lifted the dust into the air; a walking man lifted a thin layer as high as his waist, and a wagon lifted the dust as high as the fence tops, and an automobile boiled a cloud behind it ...

The wind grew stronger, whisked under stones ... marking its course as it sailed across the fields. The air and the sky darkened ... During the night the wind raced faster over the land, dug cunningly among the rootlets of the corn, and the corn fought the wind with its weakened leaves until the roots were freed by the prying wind ...

The dawn came, but no day. In the grey sky a red sun appeared, a dim red circle that gave a little light, like dusk ...

Men and women huddled in their houses, and they tied handkerchiefs over their noses when they went out, and wore goggles to protect their eyes ...

Houses were shut tight, and cloth wedged around doors and windows, but the dust came in so thinly that it could not be seen in the air, and it settled like pollen on the chairs and tables, on the dishes ...

The people came out of their houses and smelled the hot stinging air ... And the children came out of the houses, but they did not run or shout as they would have done after a rain. Men stood by their fences and looked at the ruined corn ...

As the day went forward the sun became less red. It flared down on

From John Steinbeck, *The Grapes of Wrath*, Heinemann, 1939.

the dust-blanketed land. . . . The men sat still – thinking – figuring . . .
Highway 66 is the main migrant road. 66 – the long concrete path . . .
from Mississippi to Bakersfield . . .

Sixty-six is the path of a people in flight, refugees from dust and
shrinking land, from the thunder of tractors and shrinking owner-
ship . . . from the twisting winds that howl up out of Texas . . .

B A farm in the dust bowl

A small farm in New Mexico buried by dust, 1935.

Questions

1 Use the map on page 6 to identify the states which were in the dust bowl.

2 What information in the passage helps to explain how the dust bowl was created?

3 Use a map to work out how far it is from Oklahoma to eastern California. What difficulties would the families face going west across dry areas?

4 Why might the migrants from Oklahoma not have been well received in California?

5 What clues does the photograph give about the farming activities that went on before the dust came? Why would it be difficult for the family which lived here to start farming again without help?

6 What do you think is Steinbeck's aim in this novel? Do you think it makes good evidence about this episode in American history? Can you think of other novels which tell us about a period in the history of the USA?

24 The Roosevelts

In the election of November 1932, the Democrat candidate, Franklin Delano Roosevelt, beat the Republican President, Herbert Hoover. Roosevelt was to be the only President to be elected four times and he stayed in the White House until his death in 1945. During this time he was responsible for the New Deal, which lessened the distress caused by the depression, and he led his nation in the war against Germany and Japan.

Throughout his years as President, Roosevelt had many enemies, especially among the rich and powerful, who objected to his schemes for spending public money and interfering in the running of private business. Yet he remained popular with the majority of Americans, despite the fact that the was crippled. Roosevelt had caught polio in 1921, which left him paralysed from the waist down. He went to great lengths to conceal from the public how crippled he really was. He was also greatly helped by his wife Eleanor who won support for her husband among a wide circle of influential people.

In this extract, the man who worked as usher in the White House for forty years, talks about the Roosevelts.

A President Roosevelt

For the Roosevelts, the White House was like a Grand Hotel. Eleanor Roosevelt's life was filled with visitors from early morning until late at night. . . .

I soon learned that the White House staff took extraordinary precautions to conceal Mr. Roosevelt's inability to walk. Special ramps had been built all over the White House for the President's wheelchair. . . . During State dinners, butlers seated the President first, then rolled the wheelchair out of sight. Only then were guests received in the dining room. For ceremonies in the East Room, the doormen would quietly close the double doors which were covered with red velvet curtains, after all the guests had assembled Mr. Roosevelt then rode to the doors in his wheelchair, someone lifted him from the chair, and we flung open the doors and curtains. The President on the arm of an aide, swung his legs the two steps to the podium on which he could lean whilst speaking. No photographs were permitted. . . .

On my second day in the White House, Charles Claunch, the usher on duty, took me on the elevator, to the second floor. The door opened and the Secret Service guard wheeled in the President. Startled I looked down at him. It was only then that I realized that Franklin D. Roosevelt was paralyzed. Everybody knew that the President had been stricken with infantile paralysis and his recovery was a legend, but few people were aware how completely the disease had handicapped him.

I'd seen the President once before three years earlier, when he brought his election campaign train through Creston Iowa. . . .

We all knew that he was supposed to be 'crippled' that he walked

From J. B. West, *Upstairs at the White House,* Coward, McCanne & Geoghegan Inc., 1973.

with a limp or something, but then, standing with Mrs. Roosevelt on the back platform of the campaign train, he looked strong, healthy and powerful. He had a huge head, broad shoulders and a barrel chest, and he stood well over six feet tall. I don't remember a word of his speech, but there was something in his manner. He was truly dynamic, I thought.

B Roosevelt campaigning, 1932

Meeting the people. Roosevelt during the 1932 election campaign.

Questions

1 Why should Roosevelt go to so much trouble to conceal his handicap?

2 Does the extract suggest any of the reasons why Roosevelt won four presidential elections? What other sort of information would you need to have to explain his success?

3 Does the photograph give any clues that Roosevelt was crippled?

4 What does the photograph tell you about Roosevelt's style of campaigning for elections? How might the photograph be used to help Roosevelt win votes?

5 Imagine you are Roosevelt's chauffeur. Describe, in the same way as his usher does, the measures that would need to be taken to present him to the public as active and healthy.

25 The glittering 1930s?

In March 1933, when Franklin Delano Roosevelt took the oath as President of the United States, about a quarter of the country's work force was unemployed. Roosevelt quickly introduced a series of laws, known as the 'New Deal', to take people away from the long bread lines back into jobs again.

This extract is by a high-society photographer who lived in Manhattan, one of the wealthiest parts of New York City. He was friendly with two of the President's sons, John Roosevelt and Franklin Roosevelt Junior, but he disliked their father and his 'New Deal'. He mocks the President for the way he began his radio speeches and criticises Roosevelt's treatment of his family. The passage also shows how it was possible for a pleasure-loving, wealthy American to ignore the poverty and even to disbelieve stories about people being forced to sell apples on the street or to take food from charities. The writer obviously finds it hard to understand why Roosevelt was elected for a fourth (and last) term as President.

A New York in the glittering 1930s

Franklin Roosevelt in those days we didn't even talk about. John Roosevelt and the young Franklin were great friends of mine. I photographed them in my apartment. We never did discuss the old man – ever. Well, I never liked politics. I thought the American public were so frightfully gullible to allow this man, he was a dying man, to be elected for that last term . . . O that voice!

'My dear friends . . .' You know it became such an irritation it was so patronising. It was so the great man talking down to us common little herd.

I'm sorry the boys haven't done better. And they haven't. What President's sons have? What happened to the Hoover boys? Eleanor was a great woman, making the most of everything she could out of a bad everything. But there was always admiration for her. . . .

I don't think we ever mentioned the people on relief. Friends did in private at the breakfast table or at cocktail time. But never socially. Because I always had a theory – when you're out with friends, out socially, everything must be charming, and you don't allow the ugly.

There were no apple sellers – not in New York. Never, never. There were a few beggars. One day, I saw this pathetic beggar, whom I'd always felt sorry for. This Cadillac drove up. I'd just given him a quarter and it picked him up. There was a woman driving it. And I thought: well, if they can drive a Cadillac, they don't need my quarter.

I never saw one bread line, never in New York. If they were they were in Harlem or down in Greenwich Village. They were never in this section of town.

The 'New Deal' meant absolutely nothing to me except higher taxation.

The thirties was a glamorous, glittering moment.

From Studs Terkel, *Hard Times*, Allen Lane, 1970.

B   The hungry men of New York

Unemployed men queueing for food in New York.

Questions

1 What type of people did the writer mix with?

2 Do you believe the writer when he says he never saw an apple seller or a bread line? Give reasons for your answer.

3 Why was higher taxation for the rich part of the 'New Deal'?

4 What arguments might the writer have given against the 'New Deal' laws?

5 List the objections that the writer has against Franklin Delano Roosevelt. Which of these are serious political arguments and which little more than gossip?

6 In what ways does the photograph contradict the account? Is one of these types of evidence more reliable than the other on life at this time?

7 What sort of organisation is providing the food in the photograph?

26 Unions in the 1930s

By the mid-1930s only about 3½ million American workers had joined trade unions. Most employers would not recognise unions. They refused to bargain with them over wages and conditions and tried to prevent employees joining them.

During the last weeks of 1936 workers at the General Motors factory in Flint, Michigan State, carried out a sit-in. They stayed in the plant (factory) and refused to work until General Motors agreed to recognise the UAW, the Union of Auto Workers. (The UAW was affiliated to the Congress of Industrial Organisations, CIO, one of the two large groupings of trade unions in the United States.) The Governor of Michigan, Frank Murphy, refused to use state troops, the National Guard, to force the workers out, and the strikers had much public support.

Finally an agreement was signed between Mr Knudsen, head of General Motors and John L. Lewis who was leader of the CIO. The firm agreed to recognise the UAW, which was a great triumph for the workers. The men also received a 5 per-cent increase. In the following extract the story of the strike is told by a man who was a union member at that time.

A The strike at General Motors, 1936

The Flint sit down happened Christmas Eve 1936. I was in Detroit, playing Santa Claus to a couple of small nieces and nephews. When I came back, the second shift had taken over the plant.

From Studs Terkel, *Hard Times*, Allen Lane, 1970.

Governor Murphy said he hoped to God he would never have to use the National Guard against people. But if there was damage to property, he would do so. That was right down our alley, because we invited him to the plant to see how well we were taking care of the place.

The soup kitchen was outside the plant. The women handled all the cooking, outside of one chef who came from New York. He had anywhere from ten to twenty women washing dishes and peeling potatoes in the strike kitchen. Mostly stews, pretty good meals, they were put in containers and hoisted up through the windows. The boys in there had their own plates and cups and saucers.

Time after time, people would come driving by the plant slowly. They might pull up at the kerb and roll down the window and say 'How the guys doin'?' Our guys would be lookin' out the windows, they'd be singin' and hollering.

Sometimes a guy'd come up to you in the street and say 'how the guys goin'?' You say 'Theyre doin' all right.' Then he'd give you a song and dance. 'I hear the boys at Chevrolet are gonna get run out tonight.' I'd say 'Hogwash'. He'd end with sayin' 'Well, I wish you guys the best of luck because, God damn, when I worked there it was a mess.' The guy'd turn round and walk away.

Nationally known people contributed to our strike fund. Mrs. Roosevelt for one. We even had a member of Parliament come from England and address us.

The Company tried to shut off the heat. It was a bluff. Nobody moved for half an hour, so they turned it on again. The didn't want the pipes to get cold.

The men sat in there for forty-four days. Governor Murphy was trying to get both sides to meet on some common ground. I think he lost many a good night's sleep. We wouldn't use force. Mr. Knudsen was head of General Motors, and, of course, there was John L. Lewis.

When Mr. Knudsen put his name to a piece of paper and says that General Motors recognizes the U.A.W.... Until that moment, we were non-people. We didn't even exist. That was the big one.

Questions

1 What is meant by a sit-in, or sit-down, strike?

2 Why did the workers take care not to damage the factory?

3 What evidence is there of outside support for the strikers?

4 Why would Mrs Roosevelt's support have been valuable?

5 Suggest reasons why Governor Murphy refused to break the strike by force.

6 How did the strike finish? Why did the workers see it as an important victory, 'the big one'?

7 Imagine you are taking the minutes at a meeting of directors of General Motors. Write notes on an argument between two directors, one in favour of breaking the strike, the other in favour of recognising the Union.

27 New Deal at work

In 1933 those most in need of immediate help were the 15 million unemployed. In May 1933 Congress set up a Federal Emergency Relief Administration (FERA) which made loans and gifts to states and city governments who, in turn, gave the unemployed a 'dole' – outright payments in money or grants of clothing and food.

The dole was the cheapest form of relief, but those who received it, like the Beuscher family in this extract, often lost self-respect. The New Deal began to put more emphasis on work relief schemes instead of the dole. The Civil Works Administration (CWA) was to give work to about 4 million people.

In this extract the Beuscher family from Dubuque, in the farming state of Iowa, were interviewed in 1937 as part of a government survey. The government wanted to find out how they were helped by the various New Deal Agencies.

A The Beuscher family

At home

From D. A. Shannon,
The Great Depression,
Prentice-Hall Inc., 1960.

Mr. Beuscher	62
Mrs. Beuscher	60
Paul	13
Katherine	17
Jeanette	19
Bob	21

Married and away from home

Charles	23
Celia	25
Butch	26
Eileen	28
Helen	30
Caroline	32

In the Spring of 1931, the Beuschers found themselves with a mortgaged home, four children still largely dependent on the parents and no regular income.

As they 'look back on it', Mr. and Mrs. Beuscher scarcely know how they did manage to get along during the time that they had no regular work. The irregular income from Mrs. B.'s sewing continued, though she was forced to lower prices until earnings averaged no more than $3 or $4 a week . . .

For a year after Mr. B. lost his job, the family's only cash income was the four hundred, seventy-odd dollars obtained from the insurance policies and Mrs. B.'s irregular earnings, as contrasted with the pre-depression, regular income of about $130 a month . . .

After talking things over, Mr. and Mrs. Beuscher agreed that application for relief was a virtual necessity. Mr. B. remembers going down to the court house for the first time as the hardest thing he ever had to do in his life; his hand was 'on the door-knob five times' before he turned it. . . . Soon Mr. B was assigned as a laborer to county relief work, for which he was paid, always in grocery orders, $7.20 a week . . .

While the relief grants continued, a married daughter whose husband, as a collection agent, found his commission going lower and lower, and a married son, who 'hadn't a sign of a job', moved in with the parents. There were then 13 living in the 7 room house.

The family's garden, for which the city furnished some of the seeds and the plot of ground on the city island, added fresh vegetables to the list of staples . . .

The family received food orders for only a few months, as Mr. B was soon assigned to the C.W.A. Eagle Point Park project as a laborer, earning 40 cents an hour. . . .

Bob tried at various times to be assigned to a C.C.C. camp. The family does not fully understand the many delays, though they believe that boys from smaller family groups were sent in preference to Bob because other families were more demanding and insistent than the B's. But Bob's turn finally came in the fall of 1935. . . .

Questions

1 Write a letter in which Mrs Beuscher explains the struggles the family faced before they applied for relief.

2 Why did Mr Beuscher find going to the court house the hardest thing he had ever done?

3 Why do you think Mr Beuscher was paid in grocery orders in his first relief job? In what ways would he have been better off working at Eagle Point Park?

4 Why did the married children move in with their parents? Why would many other people with city jobs go back to relatives in rural areas?

5 Work relief involved many problems for the organisers. Which ones are suggested at the end of the passage? Which others can you think of?

28 A CCC worker

The New Deal measures which Roosevelt's administration introduced included a number of relief measures. Roosevelt preferred work relief to dole payments as a means of seeing that the unemployed had enough to provide food and shelter for their families.

In April 1935, the Civilian Conservation Corps (CCC) was created. It employed young men from needy families. Over 1½ million youths were put to work in various outdoor conservation schemes.

In this extract, written in August 1935, Luther C. Wandall, a black youth from New York City, describes his experiences in the CCC.

A The Civilian Conservation Corps

According to instructions, I went Monday morning at 8 o'clock to Pier 1, North River. There were, I suppose more than 1,000 boys standing about the pier. . . .

The colored boys were a goodly sprinkling of the whole. A few middle-aged men were in evidence. These, it turned out, were going as cooks. A good many Spaniards and Italians were about. . . .

We answered questions, and signed papers, and then a group of us marched over to U.S. Army headquarters on Whitehall Street in charge of an Army officer.

Here we stopped for a complete physical examination. . . . We reached Camp Dix [New Jersey]. . . . As we rolled up in front of headquarters an officer came to the bus and told us: 'You will double time as you leave this bus, remove your hat when you hit the door, and when you are asked questions, answer "Yes sir", and "No sir".' . . .

Before we left the bus the officer shouted emphatically: 'Colored boys fall out in the rear.' The colored from several buses were herded together, and stood in line until after the white boys had been registered and taken to their tents. . . .

We were taken to a permanent camp in the Upper South. This camp was a dream compared with Camp Dix. There was plenty to eat, and we slept in barracks instead of tents . . . At the 'rec' [recreation hall] we have a radio, a piano, a store called a 'canteen', a rack of the leading New York papers. . . . We have a baseball team, boxing squad, etc. An orchestra has been formed, and classes in various arts and crafts. . . .

During the first week, we did no work outside camp, but only hiked, drilled and exercised. Since then we have worked five days a week, eight hours a day. Our bosses are local men, Southerners, but on the whole I have found nothing to complain of. The work varies, but it is always healthy, outdoor labor. . . .

Discipline is maintained by imposing extra duty and fines on offenders. The fines are taken only from the $5 a month which the men receive directly [the rest of the money, about $30, being sent home].

From W. L. Katz, *Eyewitness: the Negro in American History*, Pitman Publishing Corporation, 1967.

B The New Deal

From *Washington Star*, 26 May 1938

'Ring around a Roosevelt, Pockets full of Dough': a cartoonist's view of the New Deal in 1938

Questions

1 What does Wandall tell you about life in Fort Dix at the Southern CCC camp?

2 Why might blacks, Spaniards and Italians be a large percentage of those seeking work in 1935?

3 Why do you think the discipline was so hard in CCC camps?

4 Roosevelt believed that working on relief schemes was preferable to living on unemployment money. Can you think of reasons for this view?

5 Look carefully at the cartoon:
(a) What do the initials on the children's backs stand for?
(b) What is the difference between the people described in the passage and those shown being helped in the cartoon?
(c) Are there any similarities between the image of Roosevelt presented here and that in Source 24?
(d) Is the cartoon for or against the New Deal? Give reasons for your answer.

Part 7

★★★★★★★★★★★★★★★★★★★★★★★★★★★★
The USA and World War Two

29 Roosevelt, Churchill and Lend Lease

By 1940 the leaders of both political parties in the United States favoured aid to Britain. Roosevelt won the presidential election of that year and the Democrats strengthened their majorities in both houses of the Congress (the House of Representatives and the Senate). After the election, the defeated Republican candidate, Wendell L. Wilkie, called for national unity and support of Roosevelt's policy to aid Britain against the Fascist dictatorships.

The British government, led by Winston Churchill, was running short of war equipment. Roosevelt proposed that the United States give arms to Hitler's enemies in the same way that someone would lend 'a length of garden hose' when a neighbour's house was on fire.

To find out Britain's requirements, Roosevelt sent his most trusted adviser, Harry Hopkins, to meet Churchill in January 1941. The result of this visit was the Lend Lease Act which was passed by both houses of Congress on 11 March. It allowed the USA to lend, lease and transfer military goods and aid to Britain.

The following passage is taken from a book written by Roosevelt's son.

A Hopkins and Churchill

Hopkins had reached London persuaded that Churchill considered himself to be 'the greatest man in the world' but he rapidly fell under the spell of the tempestuous old war-horse. They got along so famously that he cabled for permission, readily granted, to stay on in England until the middle of February, six weeks in all. Most evenings, after a glass or two of sherry, they dined together in a little basement room under Number 10 Downing Street, while Churchill poured out his hopes and schemes along with the wine and vintage port. He introduced Harry to King George, who had him to lunch in Buckingham Palace. . . . He [Winston] conducted Harry on a cross country tour to show him bomb damage, defense works. . . . He plied him simultaneously with war secrets and the astounding assortment of alcohol – scotch, brandy, and champagne – that kept Winston going through the day. To the alarm of the FBI men detailed to keep tabs on him, Harry would leave some of these confidential reports scattered around his hotel bedroom until he came to learn better.

He was won over completely, as the incoming flow of his letters and cablegrams to Father demonstrated, each more fervently pro-British

From E. Roosevelt and J. Brough, *Rendezvous with Destiny*, W. H. Allen & Co. 1977.

than the last, extolling Churchill and forwarding his shopping lists for weapons and war supplies. . . .

Father was not waiting for passage of lend-lease – the Senate voted 60 to 31 in favor on March 8 – to push all pending requisitions through to the British or to weave together the strands of Anglo-American co-operation. London teemed with Americans in and out of uniform. British brains were being enlisted to work on the exploration of atomic energy. Staff talks with the British in Washington, under way since the end of January, were at the point of producing the first plans for combined strategy on the assumption that both countries would ultimately be involved in fighting with Germany and Japan. Military intelligence was being pooled. RAF bomber crews were undergoing secret instruction at United States airfields. G-men and their transatlantic counterparts were jointly checking on spying and sabotage by Nazi agents here and overseas.

Questions

1 What evidence is there that London was being heavily bombed at this time?

2 What evidence is there that Roosevelt was keen to get very close Anglo-American co-operation *before* lend lease was ratified?

3 What forms of co-operation were under way in the spring of 1941?

4 Does the passage give any clues about why Roosevelt was so active in helping Britain?

5 Compare this account with Source 13. What similarities and differences can you see in the American attitude in the early years of World War One and the early years of World War Two?

30 Pearl Harbour

On 7 December 1941 two American radar operators were surprised to see a mass of 'blips' on their screens. Their officer, however, told them not to worry. Those 'blips' were in fact the 214 Japanese planes which, in a space of a few hours, destroyed hundreds of American planes and a large part of the American Pacific Fleet as it lay in Pearl Harbour in the Hawaiian Islands. The next day a shocked and angry American Congress declared war on Japan.

This account of the attack is by an American sailor who was in the harbour on that fateful Sunday. He describes the attack on the nearby airfield and on the ships at anchor. He then tells how the local people volunteered to give blood for the American wounded. Many were Japanese, either born in Honolulu or living there as aliens.

A   An American view of Pearl Harbour

At Hickam Field, the airfield so near Pearl Harbor that is virtually the same target, a long row of hangars and bombers invited the Japanese. A bomb hit on a hangar announced the news to the thousands on the post. Men came pouring out of the barracks – men in slacks, men in shorts, some in their underwear only, some without anything on at all. What was going on? Another mock war? No, bombs! Everyone ran for clothes and then for his battle station.

I cannot tell you how many ships were lying in Pearl Harbor on that peaceful Sunday morning. That is a naval secret, But you know that Pearl Harbor is the United States largest naval base – battleships were there, destroyers lay near them, mine-layers, cruisers and all types of ships.

From somewhere a wave of torpedo planes eased down towards the ships and released their torpedoes, glittering like fish in the sun, plunging with a loud splash into the sea. Each plane had its object carefully selected in advance for the approaching planes separated and each went to a definite attack.

A massive battleship rocked as if hit by a mighty fist. Almost simultaneously jets of oil spouted all over the ship. In two minutes the deck of the ship was covered with flames. Flames leapt as high as the crows nest on which a lone sailor stood. Gropingly he leaped into the oil-covered, flaming water below, just missing the deck. When he clambered upon the beach, all the hair had been singed from his head.

At eleven o'clock Dr. Pinkerton made a short appeal over the local radio 'A call for volunteer blood donors! Report immediately to Queens Hospital.'

Some people stood in line for seven hours to give their blood. Here were Honolulu's masses – Japanese by the hundreds were there, many of them members of the local Home Defence Committee. . . .

They stood in lines of infinite patience, waiting to register a silent protest with their blood. . . .

From Blake Clark, *Pearl Harbor: An Eyewitness Account*, Bodley Head, 1940.

B A Japanese view of Pearl Harbour

A Japanese pilot drew this cartoon with a curse in English and a battle cry in Japanese: 'Hear! The voice of the moment of death. Wake up you fools.' The pilot died in the raid on Pearl Harbour.

Questions

1 What evidence is there in the extract that the Japanese attack was a well-planned surprise one?

2 Why did the Japanese attack Hickam Field first? How might the Japanese have got their information about the airfield and harbour?

3 What attitude to the raid was shown by the Japanese in the blood donor queue?

4 What does Source B tell you about the Japanese pilot who made the drawing?

5 What was the important type of ship shown in the pilot's drawing which in fact was not in Pearl Harbour at the time of the raid?

31 Hiroshima: A new horror is born

On 6 August 1945 one atomic bomb, dropped from an American B29 plane, almost wiped out the Japanese city of Hiroshima. The world's first atomic attack destroyed over three-quarters of the city's buildings and killed or wounded over half of the city's inhabitants. Some of the victims were killed immediately, others died years later from the effects of radiation.

A few days later Japan surrendered and World War Two was over. John Hersey, a New York journalist, went to the devastated city in May 1946 to find out what had happened on that fateful day.

A   The explosion

A tremendous flash of light cut across the sky. Mr. Tanimoto has a distinct recollection that it travelled from east to west, from the city toward the hills. It seemed a sheet of sun. Both he and Mr. Matsuo reacted in terror and both had time to react for they were two miles [3.2 kilometres] from the centre of the explosion.

From John Hersey, *Hiroshima*, Penguin, 1946.

Mr. Tanimoto threw himself between two big rocks – he felt a sudden pressure and then splinters and pieces of board and fragments of tile fell on him. He heard no roar.

From the mound, Mr. Tanimoto saw an astonishing panorama – as much of Hiroshima as he could see through the clouded air was giving off a thick, dreadful miasma [smell]. Houses nearby were burning, and when huge drops of water the size of marbles began to fall, he half thought that they must be coming from the hoses of firemen. (They were actually drops of condensed moisture falling from the turbulent tower of dust, heat and fission fragments that had already risen miles into the sky above Hiroshima).

Mr. Tanimoto met hundreds and hundreds who were fleeing. The eyebrows of some were burned off and slime hung from their faces and hands. Some were vomiting as they walked.

Under many houses, people screamed for help, but no one helped; in general, survivors that day assisted only their relatives or immediate neighbours. . . .

When Mr. Tanimoto reached the park, it was very crowded, and to distinguish the living from the dead was not easy, for most of the people lay still, with their eyes open. The hurt ones were quiet; no one wept, much less screamed in pain; no one complained: not even the children cried; very few people even spoke.

By nightfall, ten thousand victims of the explosion had invaded the Red Cross Hospital. Ceilings and partitions had fallen; plaster, dust, blood and vomit were everywhere. Patients were dying by the hundred, but there was nobody to carry away the corpses. . . .

A surprising number of the people of Hiroshima remained more or less indifferent about the ethics of using the bomb; 'it was war, we had to expect it' or, 'it can't be helped.'

B War in the Pacific: August 1945

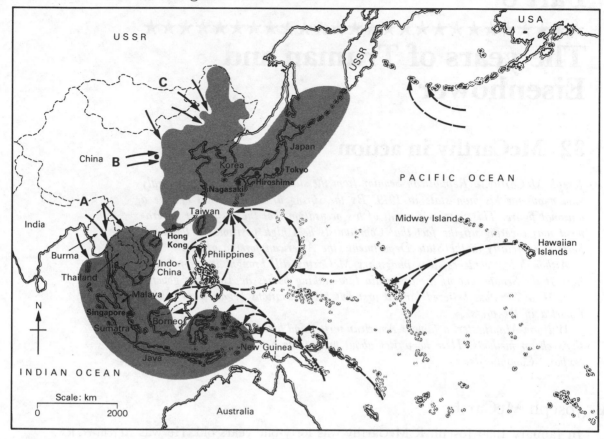

Questions

1 What could be seen or heard immediately after the bomb dropped?

2 Why do you think so few people spoke as they lay in the park?

3 What does Hersey mean by the phrase in the last paragraph, 'the ethics of using the bomb'?

4 Use the map and Sources 30 and 31A to answer these questions:
   (a) What happened in the Hawaiian Islands in December 1941?

   (b) What forces are represented on the map by the dotted arrows?

   (c) Name the armies shown at A, B and C on the map.

   (d) Which power held the territory shaded on the map in August 1945?

   (e) Do your answers to (b), (c) and (d) suggest why the Americans dropped an atomic bomb on Hiroshima in August 1945?

   (f) At what other place marked on the map was an atomic bomb dropped in 1945?

Part 8

★★★★★★★★★★★★★★★★★★★★★★★★★★

The years of Truman and Eisenhower

32 McCarthy in action

Joseph McCarthy, a Republican Senator from the state of Wisconsin, was hardly known outside his own state in 1949. By the spring of 1950 he had become a national figure. This was as a result of his accusation that the Democrat government was covering up the fact that Communists held high positions in the Civil Service, especially in the State Department (the American foreign office).

Although his 'evidence' was imaginary McCarthy still brought it before meetings of the Senate, one of the two main law-making bodies in American government. Few Senators believed him at first but his accusations began to be widely reported in the press.

William Manchester, a famous American writer and historian, detested McCarthy's cheap methods. Here he writes about one of the Senator's early efforts to 'expose' Communists.

A Joseph McCarthy

In January 1950 Joseph R McCarthy was forty-one years old. He was becoming a disgrace to the United States Senate – a cheap politician who had sunk to taking $10,000 from a manufacturer of prefabricated housing and $20,000 from the Washington lobbyist for Pepsi-Cola. He had spent it recklessly in long phone conversations with bookies. A few people knew that McCarthy's battered tan brief-case always carried a bottle of whisky. At the rate he was going, he had six, maybe seven years left.

He was a rogue, and he looked the part. His eyes were shifty. When he laughed, he snickered. His voice was a high pitch taunt. What he had going for him was a phenomenal ability to lie and an intuitive grasp of the American communications industry. That and ruthlessness. He enjoyed reading his name in the newspapers and he wanted to remain a senator. . . .

Late in the afternoon of February 20 Joe McCarthy strode out on the floor of the Senate carrying the tan briefcase, now bulging. The Democrats had demanded evidence about communists in the State Department, and twice since his return to the capital he had assured newspapermen that if he couldn't come up with it, he would resign. Now he was going to give the Senate one of the wildest evening sessions in its

From W. R. Manchester, *The Glory and the Dream*, Little, Brown & Co., 1974.

history. McCarthy stacked 81 obsolete files on his desk and those of nearby Senators. Spectators realized that McCarthy was looking at these files for the first time. He stood there almost six hours, shrugging heavily when the files baffled him but never yielding the floor. ...

Some of the 'communist' cases had nothing to do with the State Department. Number 62 was 'not important insofar as communistic activities are concerned'. ... Number 72 had the Senator baffled. 'This individual was very highly recommended as a democratic American who opposed Communism.' McCarthy plodded on doggedly. Number 9 was the same as number 77. Numbers 15, 27, 37 and 59 did not exist – they were just empty folders.

There wasn't a spy in the lot. But by inserting a phrase in a file here, deleting another here, he created the impression of subversion among those who read their newspapers by studying the comics first, then the sports page and then glancing carelessly through the headlines.

Questions

1 How does Manchester get across his opinion that McCarthy was an unreliable, shabby character?

2 How do you know from the account of the Senate meeting that McCarthy had no real evidence to back his accusations?

3 What is the writer's view of the way people came to believe McCarthy's stories about communist spying?

4 Why do you think politicians like McCarthy do sometimes get so much support?

5 What factors help politicians such as McCarthy?

33 Nixon gets out of a tight corner

Richard Milhous Nixon, a lawyer from California, first came to the American public's notice in 1949 when he helped to expose a communist spy ring inside the United States. In 1952 he was chosen as the Republicans Party's Vice-Presidential candidate. Then, just before the election, a newspaper accused Nixon of having a secret fund – suggesting he was taking bribes in return for giving favours. In fact the money was never 'secret' and was legally used for political expenses. But the Republican Presidential candidate, Dwight D. Eisenhower, was worried by the story and there was talk of Nixon being asked to resign his position.

This is an extract from Nixon's famous television speech of October 1952. He refers to his wife, Pat, and his daughters, in his reply to his critics.

A Nixon's 'Checkers' speech, 1952

My fellow Americans, I come before you tonight as a candidate for the Vice Presidency . . . and as a man whose honesty and integrity has been questioned. . . .

Not one cent of the $18, 000 ever went to me for my personal use. . . . Every penny of it was used for political expenses. . . . No contributor to this fund, no contributor to any of my campaign, has ever received any consideration that he would not have received as an ordinary constituent. . . .

I am going to give to this television and radio audience a complete financial history. . . .

I should say this – that Pat doesn't have a mink coat but Pat and I have the satisfaction that every dime that we've got is honestly ours.

We did get one gift after the election. It was a little cocker spaniel dog. Black and white spotted. And our little girl Tricia – the six year old – named it Checkers. And you know the kids love that dog and I just want to say this right now, that regardless of what they say about it, we're going to keep it.

Let me say this: I don't believe that I ought to quit, because I am not a quitter. And, incidentally, Pat is not a quitter. After all, her name is Patricia Ryan and she was born on St. Patrick's Day – and you know the Irish never quit.

But the decision, my friends, is not mine. I would do nothing that would harm the possibilities of Dwight Eisenhower to become President of the United States; and for that reason I am submitting to the Republican National Committee tonight, through this television broadcast, the decision which is theirs to make.

Let them decide whether my position will help or hurt; and I am going to ask you to help them decide. Wire and write the Republican National Committee whether I should stay or get off; and whatever their decision is, I will abide by it.

Just let me say this last word. Regardless of what happens, I am

From a speech by Richard Nixon, October 1952, reproduced in A. M. Scott and E. Wallace, *Politics USA*, Macmillan Publishing Company Inc., 1962.

going to continue this fight. I am going to campaign up and down America until we drive the crooks and Communists and those that defend them out of Washington.

And remember, folks, Eisenhower is a great man, believe me. He is a great man.

B Nixon and 'Checkers'

Senator Richard Nixon relaxes at home with the family pet, a cocker spaniel named 'Checkers'.

Questions

1 List all the parts of the speech where Nixon tries to give the impression that he is an ordinary family man. Why are there so many?

2 How might a) an independent American Republican, and b) an unmarried liberal Democrat have reacted to this broadcast?

3 Why does Nixon ask the television audience to write to the Republican National Committee?

4 How does he try to appeal to the Irish-American voters?

5 What impression does he try to create of himself as a politician?

6 The photograph was released at the same time as the broadcast was made. Why do you think Nixon agreed to this?

7 In what ways is Nixon trying to put across the same propaganda message in both the newspaper photograph and the broadcast?

34 Living like an American

The years after World War Two were generally prosperous ones for most Americans. By 1960 Americans possessed nearly half of the world's telephones and cars; and 90 per cent of Americans had a television.

After 1945 farming was highly mechanised. This brought down the price of food so families had more money left to spend on luxury goods and holidays. By 1960 virtually all workers in manufacturing industries had at least two weeks paid holiday a year.

Of all the states, California was the wealthiest. The 'Golden State' with its fruit production and oil-wells was one of the richest areas in the world.

The 1950s were a time when the USA seemed far ahead, even of those well-to-do countries in Western Europe. Even Communist countries, such as the USSR and Yugoslavia, felt they could learn something from the USA. The Soviet leader, Nikita Khrushchev, visited President Eisenhower in 1959.

In the following extract an American writer and historian, William Leuchtenberg, describes how Americans lived in the 1950s.

A The USA in the 1950s

When the Paris Editor of 'U.S. News and World Report' came home to the United States in 1960 after twelve years abroad, he was astonished at the changes. He marvelled at cocktails ready mixed in plastic envelopes and striped toothpaste. He had been living in France where only one family in ten had a bath tub with hot running water, and he was coming home to a country where, in some sections of California, at least one family in ten owned a swimming pool in the back yard.

With larger incomes than ever before there were for consumers shopping precincts with piped music, supermarkets with row on row of brilliantly coloured cartons. A Swiss Department Store chain told its customers 'live like an American'. At Uppsala, Sweden, a distinguished literary critic from an American University drew an audience of only thirty, while in the next room three hundred were listening to his wife talking about the American kitchen. Yugoslavians gathered around T.V. sets to watch 'Peyton Place'.

After Nikita Khrushchev returned from the United States in 1959 the Russian government ordered a rapid increase in the output of television sets, refrigerators and other consumer goods.

Due to much higher incomes, longer vacations and improved air transport, middle class Americans travelled to places that had long seemed the destinations only of the very rich. Families who had once counted it an adventure to take the San Francisco Ferry thought nothing of going to Venice.

In 1969 a writer observed: 'Thirty years ago the average Mid Westerner had never heard of pizza. He had never seen a foreign car or a Van Gogh reproduction. Now these things are taken for granted.'

From William E. Leuchtenberg, *A Troubled Feast: American Society since 1945*, Little, Brown & Co., 1973.

In 1952 the Eisenhower forces employed an advertising firm to sell the General, candidates became increasingly concerned about their 'image' and some of their audience assessed them as they assessed rival claims of deodorants.

Questions

1 What changes did the editor see in the USA between 1948 and 1960?

2 What do you think the Swiss department store had in mind when they encouraged people to 'live like an American'?

3 What do you think the Soviet Union's government hoped to gain by increasing the output of televisions and refrigerators after 1959?

4 In your own words, explain what is meant by selling a politician's image.

5 What effects might the wealth and affluence have had on poorer groups like the blacks in the ghettoes of Watts, Los Angeles? (see Source 40)

6 What great changes have you seen in everyday life in the past ten years?

35 The other Americans

Although after 1945 many Americans enjoyed new wealth and a higher standard of living, there was still a lot of poverty in the United States. This was especially true in inner cities and in rural areas such as the mining regions of the Appalachian Mountains in South Pennsylvania and West Virginia.

In the Appalachians poor soils made it very difficult to make a living from farming and, with many mines closing down, people were forced to move away. In the inner areas of cities such as New York, poor whites, blacks and Puerto Ricans competed for low-paid jobs.

Michael Harrington toured round the United States in the mid-1960s. Sources A and B are extracts from his book which he based on findings made during his travels. Many Americans were shocked by his observations and by figures produced by government organisations. Those in Source C give information about Americans living below the poverty line. This was calculated on the minimum amount of food needed by people, taking into account the size of family and whether they were living on farms or without land.

A   The Appalachians

Poverty is often off the beaten track. The ordinary tourist never left the main highway, and today he rides interstate turnpikes [motorways]. He does not go into the valleys of Pennsylvania where the towns look like movie sets of Wales in the thirties. He does not see the company houses in rows, the rutted roads and everything is black and dirty. And even if he were to pass through such a place by accident, the tourist would not meet the unemployed men in the bar or the women coming home from the sweatshop. The traveller comes to the Appalachian mountains in the lovely season. He sees the hills, the streams, the foliage – but not the poor. Or perhaps he looks at a run down mountain house and decides that 'those people' are truly fortunate to be free from the strains and tensions of the middle class. The only problem is that 'those people', the quaint inhabitants of those hills, are under-educated, underprivileged, lack medical care and are in the process of being forced from the land into life in the cities where they are misfits. . . .

During the fifties, 1,500,000 people left the Appalachians. Those who were left behind tended to be the older people, the less imaginative, the defeated. . . .

From Michael Harrington, *Other America*, Penguin, 1974.

B   New York City

In New York City, some of my friends call 80, Warren Street 'the slave market'.

It is a big building in downtown Manhattan. Its corridors are lined with employment agency offices; they provide the work force for the

From Michael Harrington, *Other America*, Penguin, 1974.

dishwashers and day workers, the fly-by-night jobs. It is made up of Puerto Ricans, Negroes, alcoholics, drifters and disturbed people. Some of them will pay a flat fee (usually around 10%) for a day's work. If all goes well they will make their wage. If not, they have a legal right to come back and get their half dollar. But many of them don't know that. . . .

Helpers in restaurant kitchens shift jobs rapidly and are hard to organize, this makes it a perfect place for labour and management racketeers. The dishonest union man would demand a pay off from the dishonest restaurateur. In return for this money the unionist would allow management to pay well below the prevailing union wage.

C Americans living below the poverty line

Family status and race	Number in millions below poverty line				Percentage below poverty line			
	1959	1963	1966	1968	1959	1963	1966	1968
All persons	39.5	36.4	28.5	25.4	22.4	19.5	14.7	12.8
White	28.5	25.2	19.3	17.4	18.1	15.3	11.3	10.0
Negro and other races	11.0	11.2	9.2	8.0	56.2	51.0	39.8	33.5

Figures from US Dept. of Commerce; Bureau of the Census; Current Population Reports, Series P. 60, No. 68. Reproduced in *Statistical Abstract of the United States*, 1970.

Questions

1 What is meant by company houses? What problem would face someone living in a company house when he became unemployed?

2 In which different ways does the writer suggest that the wealthier Americans did not understand the Appalachian poor?

3 If the flat 10% fee charged by the agency was usually half a dollar, what was the day's wage?

4 How did dishonest labour (or Union) officials work with racketeering managers or employers?

5 In what ways do the figures in the table support the picture of America given by Michael Harrington?

6 What do you think is meant by 'poverty line'?

7 Why was it thought important to divide the table into 'White' and 'Negro and other races'? What does the table tell you about how poverty was shared in the 1960s?

8 What other kinds of evidence would you look at if you wanted to know more about the causes of poverty in the United States?

Part 9
★★★★★★★★★★★★★★★★★★★★★★★★★★★★
Civil rights

36 Little Rock

In 1954, the highest court in the USA, the Supreme Court, ruled that states should allow blacks to attend the same schools as whites so that they could have equal opportunities and facilities.

This decision appalled many white Americans in the southern states, where state governments tried to ignore the ruling. In 1957 President Eisenhower ordered that it must be obeyed throughout the USA. Even then Governor Faubus of Arkansas decided to defy the Court and the President. On the day that a high school in Little Rock, Arkansas, was due to take in its first black students, the Governor placed state soldiers (or National Guardsmen) around it to keep them out.

As she set out for school in September 1957, Elizabeth Eckford, a sixteen-year-old black student, had little idea that Faubus would defy the President.

A Elizabeth Eckford's story

I saw a large crowd of people standing across the street from the soldiers guarding Central High School. As I walked on, the crowd suddenly got very quiet. . . .

Then someone shouted, 'Here she comes, get ready!' I moved away from the crowd on the sidewalk and into the street. If the mob came at me, I could then cross back over so the guards could protect me.

The crowd moved in closer and then began to follow me, calling me names. I still wasn't afraid. Just a little bit nervous. Then my knees started to shake all of a sudden and I wondered whether I could make it to the entrance. . . .

The crowd was quiet. I guess they were waiting to see what was going to happen. When I was able to steady my knees, I walked up to the guard who had let the white students in. When I tried to squeeze past him, he raised his bayonet and then the other guards closed in and they raised their bayonets.

They glared at me with a mean look and I was very frightened and didn't know what to do. I turned around and the crowd came toward me.

Somebody started yelling 'Lynch her!'

I tried to see a friendly face somewhere in the mob. I looked into the face of an old woman and it seemed a kind face, but when I looked at her again she spat on me.

They came closer, shouting, 'No nigger bitch is going to get in our school! Get out of here!'

From Daisy Bates, *The Long Shadow of Little Rock*, David McKay, 1962.

Then I saw a bench at the bus stop. When I got there, I don't think I could have gone another step. I sat down and the mob crowded up and began shouting all over again. Just then a white man sat down beside me, put his arm around me and patted my shoulder. He raised my chin and said, 'Don't let them see you cry'.

B Elizabeth Eckford is turned away, 4 September 1957

Questions

1 What did Elizabeth at first think the Guardsmen were there for?

2 What is meant by 'lynching'? Which 'white' society, mentioned earlier in this book, used such methods?

3 What evidence is in the extract to suggest there was some hope for the future in black–white relations in the USA?

4 Why did the question of integrated schools lead to such bitterness?

5 If you had not read Elizabeth's story, why might the photograph be misleading?

37 Black like me

By the end of the 1950s the blacks in the USA were becoming more organised in their struggle for full civil rights. A growing number of white Americans saw the justice of the black cause and joined the civil rights movement. In 1959, one of these whites, John Howard Griffin, decided to carry out an experiment. He visited New Orleans and first spent several days there as himself and then, with the aid of a friendly doctor, changed his skin colour from white to black.

In the first part of the extract Griffin describes how he retraced the visits he had made as a white; in the second part he writes about a journey on a long distance 'Greyhound' bus travelling through Mississippi.

A John Howard Griffin's experiment

New Orleans

The streetcar rumbled to a stop. I remembered to let the white man on first. He paid his fare and walked to an empty seat, ignoring me. I felt my first triumph. He had not questioned me. The ticket-taker nodded affably when I paid my fare. Though street cars are not segregated in New Orleans, I took a seat near the back. Negroes there glanced at me without the slightest suspicion or interest. . . .

From John Howard Griffin, *Black Like Me*, Catholic Book Club, 1960.

I got off and passed the same taverns and amusement places where the hawkers had solicited me on previous evenings. They were busy, urging white men to come in and see the girls. Tonight they did not solicit. Tonight they looked at me but did not see me. . . .

I went into a drug store that I had patronised every day since my arrival. I walked to the cigarette counter where the same girl I had talked with every day waited on me. She handed me some cigarettes and gave change with no sign of recognition, none of the pleasant conversation of previous days.

Again my reaction was that of a child. I was aware that the street smells, and the drug store odours of perfume were exactly the same to the Negro as they had been to the white. Only I could not order a limeade or ask for a glass of water. . . .

On the Greyhound bus to Mississippi

Among the passengers was a striking Negro man, tall, slender, elegantly dressed – the Valentino type [like Rudolph Valentino, the Italian–American film star]. He wore a moustache and a neatly trimmed Van Dyke beard. He walked towards the rear giving the whites a fawning almost tender look.

He began to shout at two Negroes behind him 'This place stinks. Damned common niggers. Look at all of them – don't know how to dress. Do you speak German? No. You're ignorant'.

He begins to speak with Griffin

'I'm not pure Negro', he said proudly 'My mother was French, my father Indian.'

'I see . . .'

'She was Portuguese, my mother – a lovely woman', he sighed. A strange, sweetish odour came from him. I supposed it to be marijuana.

Questions

1 Why did Griffin carry out his experiment?

2 What was Griffin's first 'triumph' on the streetcar (bus)?

3 Why didn't the men outside the taverns encourage Griffin to go inside?

4 What conclusions might be drawn from the drug store girl's behaviour?

5 Why could Griffin not have a glass of water or limeade?

6 In your own words describe and explain the Valentino type's behaviour to the whites and blacks on the bus.

7 What were the two main lessons about the position of black people that Griffin might have learned from this experiment?

38 Martin Luther King

The most famous campaigner for civil rights in the 1960s was Dr Martin Luther King. King had called Birmingham, Alabama, 'the most segregated city in the USA'. In April 1963 King and thousands of his supporters demonstrated against the city authorities – they 'sat in' at segregated cafes, went to 'whites only' churches and marched to City Hall.

The Birmingham police, under orders from its Commissioner, Eugene Connors, used dogs, clubs, electric cattle prods and powerful water hoses against the peaceful demonstrators.

King spent eight days in jail and in this letter he answers complaints that he was an outsider interfering in purely local affairs. He also compares his peaceful civil rights movement with the 'Black Muslim' movement which stood for total victory of the blacks over the whites and the use of violence if necessary. To show their contempt for the religion of the whites Black Muslims claimed to have adopted the Muslim faith.

A Letter from Birmingham Jail

We have waited for more than 346 years for our constitutional and God given rights. The nations of Asia and Africa are moving at jet-like speed toward gaining political independence but we still creep at horse and buggy pace toward gaining a cup of coffee at a lunch counter. Perhaps it is easy for those who have never felt the stinging darts of segregation to say 'wait'. But when you have seen vicious mobs lynch your mothers and fathers at will; when you have seen hate-filled police-men curse, kick and even kill your black brothers and sisters with im-punity; when you suddenly find your tongue twisted as you seek to explain to your six year old daughter why she can't go to the local amusement park and see tears welling up when she is told the fountain is closed to colored children; when you take a cross country drive and find it necessary to sleep night after night in the uncomfortable corners of your automobile because no motel will accept you; when you are humiliated day in and day out by nagging signs reading 'white' and 'colored'; when your first name becomes 'nigger', your middle name becomes 'boy' (however old you are) – THEN comes a time when the cup of endurance runs over.

I stand in the middle of two forces in the Negro community. One is the force of complacency made up of Negroes who, as a result of long years of oppression, are so completely drained of self respect that they have adjusted to segregation and of a few middle class Negroes who have been insensitive to the problems of the masses.

The other force is one of bitterness and hatred. The largest and best known being Elijah Muhammad's Muslim Movement. This movement is made up of people who have lost faith in America, who have given up Christianity and who have concluded that the white man is a devil.

From Martin Luther King, 'Letter from Birmingham Jail', first published in the *Christian Century Magazine*, 12 June 1963.

B The march on Washington, 1963

Civil rights marchers in Washington, August 1963. Martin Luther King is fifth from the right in the front line.

Questions

1 Which everyday examples of segregation made Martin Luther King angry?

2 Why does he make the point that countries in Asia and Africa were 'moving at jet-like speed' towards independence?

3 Which complaints of King's is similar to the youths interviewed in the Watts Riot? (Source 40)

4 What is King's view of the two groups of blacks who have adjusted to segregation?

5 How does he compare his movement with the 'Black Muslims'?

6 Which of the placards shown in the photograph support the evidence about black grievances given in Luther King's letter and Sources 36 and 37?

7 Does Martin Luther King's letter explain why whites joined in the civil rights march?

39 The boy who painted Christ black

From the Civil War until the 1950s black children in the Deep South had attended only segregated schools. These schools were usually short of staff or equipment and most blacks were doomed to sub-standard education which would hinder their chances of improving their position in America.

During the early 1960s the civil rights movement steadily gained ground. Civil rights campaigners, white and black, were demanding for blacks the basic rights that most whites enjoyed. They wanted an end to segregation in all its forms in cafés, hotels and in schools.

The civil rights movement also led to a new kind of writing; stories written by black Americans. This extract is taken from a collection published in 1966.

A A painting of Christ

He was the smartest boy in the Muskogee County School – for colored children. The teacher always pronounced his name with profound gusto as she pointed him out as the ideal student. Once I heard her say: 'If he were white he might, some day, become President'. Only Aaron Crawford wasn't white. His skin was so solid black that it glowed.

For the teacher's birthday, Aaron Crawford painted the picture that caused an uproar at the school.

The teacher sensed that Aaron had a present for her. Still smiling, he placed it on her desk and began to help her unwrap it. As the last piece of paper fell from the large frame, the teacher jerked her hand away from it suddenly, her eyes flickering unbelievingly. Temporarily, there was no other sound in the room.

The teacher turned towards the children, staring reproachfully. They did not move their eyes from the present. It was a large picture of Christ – painted black!

'Aaron,' she spoke at last, a slight tinge of uncertainty in her tone, 'this is a most welcome present. Thanks. I will treasure it. Suppose you come forward and tell the class how you came to paint this remarkable picture.'

'It was like this' he said, placing full emphasis on every word. 'You see, my uncle who lives in New York teaches Negro History. When he visited us last year he was telling me about the many great black folks who have made history. He said black folks were once the most powerful people on earth. When I asked him about Christ, he said no one ever proved whether he was black or white. Somehow a feeling came over me that he was a black man, 'cause he was so kind and forgiving, kinder than I have ever seen white men be.'

When I came close the picture, it looked more like a helpless Negro, pleading silently for mercy.

In the next week came Professor Danual. He was the supervisor of all the city schools.

From John Henrik Clarke (ed.), *American Negro Short Stories*, Hill & Wang, 1966.

He was a tall white man with solid grey hair. As he passed me, I heard the teachers, frightened, sucking in their breath.

After he sat down, the school chorus sang two spirituals and then the Supervisor began to review the array of handwork on display.

Suddenly his clear blue eyes flickered in astonishment 'Who painted this sacrilegious nonsense?' he demanded sharply.

Questions

1 In your own words explain why Aaron painted a black Jesus Christ.

2 What did the supervisor mean by calling the picture 'sacrilegious nonsense'? Can you understand why he was so shocked and angry?

3 Why do you think Aaron's uncle taught him about famous black people in history?

4 Find a picture of Christ and try to explain what was in the artist's mind when he drew or painted it.

5 Why would a black writer involved in the civil rights movement use this subject for his story?

6 What effect might the story have on a supporter and on an opponent of black civil rights?

40 Watts, 1965

In the mid-1960s there were many outbreaks of protest by blacks, especially the younger ones, against the poor housing, health and education and the high rates of unemployment in their inner city districts. Relations with the police became extremely bitter. Watts was a black district in the wealthy city of Los Angeles; of the 205 police in the Watts force only 5 were black. On 11 August 1965, in the middle of a heat wave, a policeman arrested a black youth. A scuffle took place with the boy's mother but wild rumours spread and soon the area became the scene of riots.

During the 6 days of rioting, 34 people were killed, mainly blacks; 1,032 people were injured; 4,000 arrests were made and over 40 million dollars worth of property was damaged.

The extract below is part of a report from a Commission set up by Governor Brown of California to investigate the causes of the riots.

A Report on the Watts riots, 1965

12 August 1965

By 12.20 a.m. approximately 50 to 75 youths were on either side of Avalon Boulevard at Imperial Highway, throwing missiles at passing cars and the police used vehicles with red lights and sirens to disperse the crowd. Some of the older citizens in the area were inquiring, 'what are those crazy kids doing?' A number of adult Negroes expressed the opinion that the police should open fire on the rock throwers to stop their activities. It was estimated that by 12.30 a.m. 70% of the rioters were children and the remainder were young adults and adults. Their major activity was throwing missiles at passing vehicles driven by whites.

Witnesses stated at this time: 'I'm throwing rocks because I'm tired of a white man misusing me'. 'Man, this is the part of town they have given us, and if they don't want to be killed they had better keep their — out of here'. 'The cops think we are scared of them because they got guns, but you can only die once; if I got a few of them I don't mind dying.'

Sunrise disclosed five burned automobiles, amidst a large amount of rubble, broken bricks, stones and shattered glass around Imperial Highway.

As an indication of the mood of the crowd of approximately 400 persons who had gathered next morning, the following comments of the youths in the crowd are quoted:

'Like why, man, should I get home? These cops have been pushin' me around all my life. Kickin my — and things like that. Whitey ain't no good. He talked about law and order, it's his law and order, it ain't mine.'

'If I've got to die, I ain't dyin' in Vietnam, I'm going die here.'

'I don't have no job. I ain't worked for two years – he, the white

From a Report by the McCohen Commission, reproduced in R. Hofstadter, and M. Wallace, *American Violence: A Documentary History*, Alfred A. Knopf Inc., 1960.

man, got everything, I ain't got nothing. What you expect me to do? I get my kicks when I see Whitey running. . . .'

'Whitey use his cops to keep us here. We are like hogs in a pen. . . .'

13 August

The owner of a liquor store at East 103rd Street was reported to have barricaded himself in his store and to have shot persons attempting to break in.

Business buildings on 103rd Street were burned completely and firemen driven off by uncontrolled rioters.

14 August

At 5: 15 a.m. Powel Harbin was shot and killed by police as a looter.

Questions

1 As the introduction says, this riot began with a single scuffle. What reasons are given in the passage for its spreading so widely?

2 In what ways does this extract support Martin Luther King's view (Source 38) that some blacks accepted their poor social conditions?

3 What do you learn about the relations between some young blacks and some older blacks?

4 What do you think the black youth meant by saying that they were 'like hogs [pigs] in a pen'?

5 Many of those interviewed blamed the police. Do you think this was completely, partly, or not at all fair? Give reasons for your answer.

Part 10

★★★★★★★★★★★★★★★★★★★★★★★★★★★★
War and politics in the '60s and '70s

41 The presidential election, 1960

In the Autumn of 1960 the Republican Richard Nixon and the Democrat John Fitzgerald Kennedy were campaigning for the November presidential election. Richard Nixon, had already been the Vice-President and was a very experienced politician. His party had a great deal of support from big business but also seemed to be favoured by a majority of the middle classes, farmers and the people of the small towns in the Mid-West.

John Fitzgerald Kennedy, the Democrat candidate, had support from the trade unions, Irish-Americans and many blacks, and he could use his father's great wealth for campaign funds.

Kennedy was a senator but was younger and less experienced than Nixon. He was also a Roman Catholic and no Catholic had ever been elected President. But he overcame this disadvantage and won by a tiny majority. Many experts believed that it was the four television debates between the two rivals that gave Kennedy victory. In the following extract from his book on the election Theodore H. White describes the first debate and discusses the part television played in the election.

From Theodore H. White, *Making of the President, 1960,* Atheneum Publishers, 1961.

A   The power of television

There was, first and above all, the overwhelming impression that side by side the two seemed evenly matched – and this was for Kennedy a major victory. Until the cameras opened on the Senator and the Vice-President, Kennedy had been the boy under assault and attack by the Vice-President as immature, young, inexperienced. Now, obviously, in flesh and behaviour he was the Vice-President's equal.

Tonight Kennedy was calm and nerveless in appearance. The Vice-President, by contrast, was tense, almost frightened and, occasionally, haggard looking to the point of sickness, his 'lazy-shave' powder faintly streaked with sweat, his eyes exaggerated hollows of blackness, his jaw, jowls and face dropping with strain.

Nixon's T.V. advisers had been told that the studio background would be grey, a relatively dark tone; therefore they urged Nixon to dress in a light grey suit for contrast. Yet the background was lighter than they had anticipated and they insisted, rightly, it be repainted – but each time it was repainted the grey tone dried light. Against this light background Nixon, in his light grey suit, faded into a fuzzed out-line while Kennedy in his dark suit had the crisp picture edge of contrast.

There was, lastly, the fact that the Vice-President had still not recovered from his illness and was unrested from the exertions of his first two weeks of intense campaigning.

All this, however, was unknown to the national audience. Those who heard the debates on radio, according to sample surveys, believed that the two candidates came off almost equal. Yet every survey of those who watched on television indicated that the Vice-President had come off poorly.

What did the debates do? There is a survey by Dr. Elino Roper – he estimated 2 million of Kennedy's voters came from television impact on their minds, and since Kennedy won by only 112,000 votes, he was entirely justified in stating on the Monday following election November 12th:

'It was T.V. more than anything else that turned the tide.'

Questions

1 How did the fact that the debate was held at all help Kennedy?

2 What do you think is meant by 'lazy-shave' powder?

3 Can you account for the differences between the effects of radio and television?

4 Make a list of ways in which British politicians arrange their television appearances to gain support from viewers.

5 What three kinds of evidence are there that Kennedy gained support from the debates being televised?

42 John F. Kennedy

John Fitzgerald Kennedy took the oath of President on 20 January 1961, the first United States President to be born in the twentieth century. He promised to create a new, vigorous style of government and to prove that government was concerned for civil rights and the poor.

This extract by the American historian, William Manchester, describes the first hectic days of Kennedy's presidency and shows how Kennedy created an impression of a new type of politician with his beautiful wife, young family and football-loving brother, Robert. His brother was Attorney General, the member of the government in charge of courts and the legal system.

A The Kennedy presidency

Noticing that there were no blacks among the cadets in the inaugural, parade, he started an official enquiry on the spot. . . . The next morning he was sending off Executive Order No 1 to double the food rations of four million needy Americans. 'He did everything today except climb up the Washington Monument' wrote a reporter of one of those early days.

The rest of Washington was expected to keep pace with him. 'The deadline for everything is the day before yesterday', said the new Secretary of Labor. There was to be a dynamic policy of action, typified by the new Secretary of Labor, who settled a strike during his first twenty-four hours in office. One Secretary was observed simultaneously signing his mail, carrying on a telephone conversation, and relaying instructions to an aide by crude semaphore; and a member of the cabinet, Robert McNamara, startled Pentagon guards by showing up at 7.30 each morning.

Two months after taking the oath Kennedy had issued thirty-two official messages and legislative recommendations (Eisenhower had issued five) while delivering twelve speeches, sending twenty-eight communications to foreign chiefs of state, and holding seven press conferences. Reporters were fascinated: more of them came than for the conferences of any other President before or since. No details seemed too small for him. At one early press conference he answered in the knowledgeable way a question about a proposal to ship $12,000,000 in Cuban molasses to the United States – information which had appeared four days earlier near the bottom of a departmental report. . . .

The Kennedy image was forming; a combination of Jacqueline Kennedy's beauty, three year old Caroline's charm, the elegant rhetoric of the President's speeches, the football on Robert Kennedy's desk, and the new idealism.

From William Manchester, *The Glory and the Dream*, Little, Brown & Co., 1974.

B The Kennedy family

John Kennedy, photographed in 1959, with his wife and small daughter.

Questions

1 In your own words list seven examples of the way Kennedy and his government showed they were hard and quick workers.

2 What effects might these first days of the Presidency have had on the American people?

3 Is there any evidence in this extract that Kennedy might be able to bring about real changes in the lives of the American people, rather than simply a new style in government?

4 In the light of this passage, say what you think is meant by the phrase, 'the Kennedy image'. What types of people might be attracted or annoyed by this image?

5 Describe in your own words how the photograph of the Kennedy family would contribute to the Kennedy image.

43 Crisis over Cuba

On 20 January 1961 John Fitzgerald Kennedy became President of the United States. He was soon challenged by Nikita Khrushchev who had been leader of the Soviet government since 1955.

On 16 October 1962 Kennedy was informed for the first time that launching sites for Soviet inter-continental ballistic missiles (ICBMs) were being set up on the island of Cuba, just 145 kilometres from the American mainland (see map).

The extract is taken from a book by William Manchester, a well-known American writer and historian. It describes the meetings of the politicians who sat on the Executive Committee (Ex Comm) of the National Security Council, which had to advise the President on military action in the Cuban Crisis. Among them were Robert McNamara and Robert Kennedy (the younger brother of the President).

A   The blockade

Wednesday October 17

. . . Majority opinion still favours an air attack. McNamara proposes an alternative: a naval blockade of Cuba. Bombing and blockading are both acts of war, but the blockade has the advantage of avoiding bloodshed at least in its first stages. An air strike would kill about 25,000 Cubans and an undetermined number of Soviet technicians. If Russians die, total war with the Soviet Union will be almost inevitable. . . .

Thursday October 18

The U.S. intelligence estimates that the weapons now in Cuba constitute about half the I.C.B.M. [missile] capacity of the entire Soviet Union. If they are fired, eighty million Americans will be dead in a few minutes. According to the latest Intelligence reports the first missiles could be ready for launching in eighteen hours. . . .

A legal adviser suggests it might be better if the blockade were called a quarantine. The weight of opinion is moving towards this choice. Robert Kennedy is strongly in favour of it. With the memory of Pearl Harbor, he says, the United States cannot launch a surprise air attack in which thousands of innocent people would die. . . .

Friday October 19

The Ex Comm is in continuous session all day Friday and all Friday night. Now there is a clear majority for the blockade.

Saturday October 20

. . . The President makes the final decision in favour of the blockade. The B-52 Bomber force has been ordered into the air fully loaded with atomic weapons. . . .

Monday October 22

. . . Kennedy's speech begins at 7 p.m. on all T.V. Channels. . . . He warns Khrushchev: any missile launched from Cuba will be regarded as an attack by the Soviet Union on the United States, requiring full retaliatory response against the U.S.S.R.

From William Manchester, *The Glory and the Dream*, Little, Brown & Co., 1974.

B The area of conflict 1962

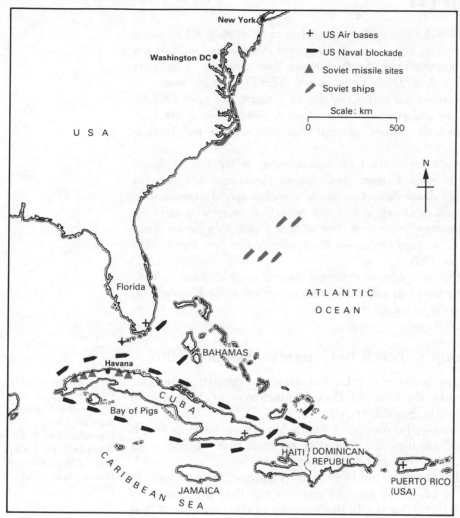

The Cuban Crisis 1962

Questions

1 Look carefully at the extract and the map and explain why the Americans were so concerned about the Soviet missile launching sites in Cuba.

2 Why do you think the legal adviser suggested that it would be better to use the word 'quarantine' rather than 'blockade'?

3 Why were McNamara and Kennedy in favour of a blockade rather than an air attack on Cuba? What did Robert Kennedy have in mind when he spoke of Pearl Harbour?

4 Why did the Soviet leaders choose Cuba and not any of the other islands on this map?

44 Vietnam (1)

After the French had been defeated in South-East Asia in 1954, the USA became a major influence in that area. The United States offered economic and military aid to non-Communist governments in South Vietnam and organised a military alliance, the South-East Asia Treaty Organisation (SEATO), in the area.

In 1962 the United States had only 4,000 men in Vietnam, but after 1964 the build-up of American air and ground forces accelerated. Bombings of North Vietnam were stepped up as the Johnson administration tried to force the North to peace talks.

The Johnson administration justified the war according to the domino theory. This theory held that if South Vietnam should become Communist then one after another the countries of South-East Asia would be taken over by communism. Military action was said to be only a first step to make it possible to carry out schemes for economic recovery in the area. One of these was a plan for an Asian Development Bank, put forward by Eugene Black after he had been sent to Vietnam by the President in 1965.

In January 1967 President Johnson explained these ideas in a speech to Congress. Only a year later there was such widespread opposition to the Vietnam War that Johnson decided not to stand for re-election.

A President Johnson's speech to Congress, January 1967

We are in Viet-Nam because the United States of America and our allies are committed by the SEATO Treaty to 'act to meet the common danger' of aggression in Southeast Asia. . . .

We are there because the people of South Viet-Nam have as much right to remain non-Communist – if that is what they choose – as North Viet-Nam has to remain Communist. . . .

You will remember that we stood in Western Europe 20 years ago. Is there anyone in this Chamber tonight who doubts that the course of freedom was not changed for the better because of the courage of that stand?

Sixteen years ago we and others stopped another kind of aggression – this time it was in Korea. . . . The Asia of tomorrow will be far different because we have said in Viet-Nam, as we said 16 years ago in Korea: 'This far and no further'. . . .

Our South Vietnamese allies are also being tested tonight. Because they must provide real security to the people living in the countryside. And this means reducing the terrorism and the armed attacks, which kidnapped and killed 26,900 civilians in the last 32 months, to levels where they can be successfully controlled by the regular South Vietnamese security forces. It means bringing to the villagers an effective civilian government that they can respect, and that they can rely upon, and that they can participate in, and that they can have a personal stake in. . . .

From a speech by President Johnson delivered to Congress 10 January 1967, reproduced in A. E. Campbell, *The USA in World Affairs*, George Harrap & Co. Ltd., 1974.

As recommended by the Eugene Black mission, and if other nations will join us, I will seek a special authorization from the Congress of $200 million for East Asian regional programs.... The moment that peace comes...I will ask the Congress for funds to join in an international program of reconstruction and development for all the people of Viet-Nam – and their deserving neighbors who wish our help. ... Let us remember that we have been tested before and America has never been found wanting.

So with your understanding, I would hope your confidence and your support, we are going to persist – and we are going to succeed.

Questions

1 Explain what was in Johnson's mind when he spoke of (a) Europe twenty years before and (b) Korea sixteen years earlier? In what ways were these two struggles different?

2 What is the main job that Johnson suggests the troops will have to do in Vietnam?

3 What sort of schemes would be included in a 'program of reconstruction and development'?

4 What sentiments of the American people is the President hoping to play on in this extract?

45 Vietnam (2)

By 1968 more than half a million American troops were fighting in South Vietnam. They were far more heavily armed than the South Vietnam soldiers who were known as (ARVNs).

The Americans' main enemy turned out to be the Vietcong (VC), a force of guerrilla fighters operating in the South. Some were men sent in from the North, others were southern people fighting to get rid of an unpopular and corrupt government. The Vietcong were often sheltered by South Vietnamese villagers, sometimes out of fear and sometimes from sympathy for their cause. The Americans often found themselves attacking and killing civilians who were not Vietcong soldiers.

In the late 1960s an American writer, Murray Polner, interviewed young Americans who had fought in the war to see if the brutal experience had any permanent effects on them and their families. To protect these ex-soldiers, their names were altered. 'Mike Pearson' had received medals for bravery in Vietnam, but on his return to the USA he joined in demonstrations against the war.

A   A soldier's story

One day, Mike Pearson suddenly stood up in his living room and said 'I can't sleep, I'm a murderer'.

'We were outside Bac Lieu' he went on, 'My God, how I remember that damned day. Hot and sticky – the mosquitoes were drivin' me crazy. And there was this little boy, about eight or nine. He was climbin' out of a tree. I grabbed him and blurted out in Vietnamese – what little I know – "who are you and what're you doin' here?" He was afraid of me and pulled away. He had his hand behind his back like he was hidin' something', "grab him" someone screamed, "he's got somethin'". I made a move for him and his hand moved again; "shoot" – because of my training, because of what my officer-in-charge told me to do, and because I was afraid and this was the first enemy I had come across, I fired at him. Again and again, until I emptied my whole M-2 carbine chamber at him. When I looked again he was cut in two, with his guts all around. I vomited. I wasn't trained for that – it was out and out murder. They're the enemy, but they're fighting for their country. When I told the psychiatrist and the Catholic Chaplain, they said I was only doing my duty – My duty? You know, that little boy had a three inch penknife, and I had a carbine. . . .

'Another time, in a village, a woman ran out of her hut with a rifle held high above her head. She wasn't shooting it, only carryin' it high, and cryin' like she was mad. She was old, like my grandmother maybe. One of the ARVNs then began shouting "VC! VC!" I fired once, twice. She fell dead. You know I killed nine people – fighting for their country against us and our stooges [South Vietnamese]. Killin' came easy after that.

'My family and everybody I knew, believed in the glory of the country. . . . We were to do what our leaders wanted us to do. So I never wanted to think about Vietnam. But I was forced to.'

From Murray Polner, *No Victory Parades*, Orbach & Chambers, 1971.

B A soldier's duty

South Vietnamese women and children are kept under guard by an American soldier.

Questions

1 Can you explain why Mike shot the young Vietnamese boy?

2 What conflict was there between the way Mike had been brought up and his views on the Vietnam War?

3 Write the script for a family discussion about Vietnam between people who have read this book and heard President Johnson's speech (Source 44) on TV.

4 Look carefully at the photograph and answer the following questions.
  (a) What was the photographer trying to convey to the general public by this particular photograph?
  (b) How might the general public in the USA have reacted to this photograph?
  (c) Does the photograph tell you anything of the photographer's own views about the Vietnam War?

46 Nixon in Communist China

Ever since the Communist People's Republic of China (PRC) was set up in 1949 relations between China and the USA had been very poor. In 1971 relations began to improve. It was clear to both China and the USA that the Soviet Union was their common enemy. But both governments were cautious about changing their policies too suddenly and too openly. First, the Chinese invited an American table tennis team to their country. The next month, President Nixon received a message from the President of Pakistan suggesting that the Chinese leadership might welcome a visit to their country.

In his memoirs, Richard Nixon describes how his National Security Adviser, Henry Kissinger, made a secret visit to Peking in July 1971. Later, in February 1972, Nixon, his wife, Pat, and Henry Kissinger made a public visit to China and were received by the Chinese leader, Chou En-lai. In the last two paragraphs of this section, Nixon tells how he and Henry Kissinger handled the tricky question of telling the American people about the results of their visit.

A Kissinger's visit to China, July 1971

We arranged that Kissinger would fly to Vietnam for consultations early in July and then stop in Pakistan on the way back. There he would develop a stomach ache that would require him to stay in bed and not be seen by the press. Then with President Yahya's co-operation, he would fly over the mountains into China. The stomach ache was scheduled for July 9–11. Kissinger would then fly to San Clemente to report to me.

From Richard M. Nixon, *The Memoirs of Richard Nixon*, Grosset & Dunlap Inc., 1978.

Kissinger's trip was given the codename Polo – after Marco Polo, another Western traveler who made history by journeying to China....

Because of the need for complete secrecy and the lack of any direct communications facilities between Peking and Washington, I knew that we would have no word from Kissinger while he was in China. Even after he had returned to Pakistan it would still be important to maintain secrecy, so before Kissinger left, we agreed on a single codeword – Eureka – which he would use if his mission were successful and the presidential trip had been arranged.

B Nixon's visit to China, February 1972

The arrival

Our plane landed smoothly, and a few minutes later we came to a stop in front of the terminal. The door was opened and Pat and I stepped out.

From Richard M. Nixon, *The Memoirs of Richard Nixon*, Grosset & Dunlap Inc., 1978.

Chou En-lai stood at the foot of the ramp, hatless in the cold. Even a heavy overcoat did not hide the thinness of his frail body. When we were about halfway down the steps, he began to clap. I paused for a moment and then returned the gesture, according the Chinese custom.

I knew that Chou had been deeply insulted by Foster Dulles's refusal to shake hands with him at the Geneva Conference in 1954. When I reached the bottom step, therefore, I made a point of extending my hand as I walked toward him. When our hands met, one era ended and another began. . . .

Later meetings with Chinese leadership

While I was in these meetings with Chou, Pat carried out a full schedule that included visits to the Peking Zoo and the Summer Palace. When we met at the guest house that evening, she remarked that although the Chinese she had met were gracious and eager to cooperate, she felt that our reception was somehow restrained. She had been kept from meeting people and the only contact she had had with anyone other than the official guides was on a visit to the kitchen of the Peking Hotel. We discussed the tremendous problems our visit presented to the Chinese leadership. . . . Two decades of virulent anti-American propaganda could not be undone overnight and the Chinese masses would take time to assimilate the new line emanating from Peking. . . .

We [Kissinger and Nixon] knew that if the Chinese made a strongly belligerent claim to Taiwan in the communiqué, I would come under murderous cross-fire from any or all the various pro-Taiwan, anti-Nixon, and anti P.R.C. lobbies and interested groups at home. If these groups found common ground on the eve of the presidential elections, the entire China initative might be turned into a partisan issue. . . .

Our joint statement, issued from Shanghai at the end of the trip, has become known as the Shanghai Communiqué . . . the communiqué broke diplomatic ground by stating frankly the significant difference between the two sides on major issues rather than smoothing them over.

Questions

1 Why should so much trouble be taken to make Kissinger's first visit secret?

2 Can you think of any reasons why Pakistan should be willing to act as a go-between?

3 What reasons did Pat and Richard Nixon work out for their 'restrained' reception?

4 In your own words, explain why Nixon and Kissinger felt they had to state the differences between the two sides in the communiqué?

5 What would be the advantages and disadvantages arising from the China trip for Nixon's political position in the USA?

47 Watergate

As the November Presidential elections of 1972 drew nearer, tens of millions of dollars were collected for a secret, illegal fund to help Richard Nixon be re-elected.

In March high-ranking White House officials allowed some of that money to be paid to George Liddy and Howard Hunt to organise a break-in and bugging at the Watergate Hotel in Washington DC, the Democrat Party's headquarters.

On 18 June 1972 the burglars were arrested and nearly half a million dollars was paid over the next few months to keep the burglars from talking about their connection with the White House.

On 30 April 1973 President Nixon, in a nationwide television broadcast, said that facts about the break-in (which had been discovered by two journalists) had been concealed from him.

However, Nixon could not avoid the Watergate issue; in May 1973 a Senate Committee began its televised hearings on the Watergate scandal; Nixon was forced to hand over tapes of conversations he had had with key people in the affair. Here are two extracts from the tapes of 21 March 1973 when Nixon and John Dean first discuss the money being paid out for the cover-up and later talk about the problem of perjury – the lies the conspirators had told to the courts.

The main people involved were:

John Dean: Counsel (Adviser) to the President
John D. Ehrlichman: Assistant to the President for Domestic Affairs
H. R. Haldeman: Assistant to the President; White House Chief of Staff
Charles (Chuck) Colson: Special Counsel to the President
Egil (Bud) Krogh: Assistant to Ehrlichman
Jeb Magruder: Deputy Campaign Director – Committee to Re-elect the President
John N. Mitchell: Campaign Director – Committee to Re-elect the President; Attorney General in 1972
The Cubans: The Watergate Burglars; some were Cubans

A The Watergate tapes

Dean: ... We have a cancer within, close to the Presidency, that is growing. ... Basically it is because (1) we are being blackmailed (2) people are going to start perjuring themselves very quickly to protect other people in the line ... there is the problem of the continued blackmail which will not only go on now but it will go on while these people are in prison ... will cost money. It is dangerous. ... We just don't know about those things, because we are not criminals and not used to dealing in that business.

President: That's right.

Dean: It is a tough thing to know how to do.

President: Maybe it takes a gang to do that.

Dean: That's right. Plus there is a real problem in raising money. Mitchell has been working on raising money. He is one of the ones with the most to lose. But there is no denying the fact that the White House,

From the tapes of 21 March 1973, reproduced in R. B. Morris & J. L. Woodress, *Voices from America's Past, vol. 4: Years of National Turmoil*, E. P. Dutton & Co. Inc., 1976.

in Ehrlichman, Haldeman and Dean, are involved in some of the early money decisions.

President: How much money do you need?

Dean: I would say these people are going to cost a million dollars over the next two years.

President: . . . you could get a million dollars. You could get it in cash. I know where it could be gotten. But the question is who the hell would handle it? Any ideas on that?

The problem of perjury

Dean: . . . Bud Krogh in his testimony before the Grand Jury, was forced to perjure himself. He is haunted by it.

President: What did he perjure himself on, John?

Dean: Did he know the Cubans – He did.

President: He said he didn't?

Dean: That is right. They didn't press him hard.

President: He might be able to – I am just trying to think. Perjury is an awful hard thing to prove. If he could just say that I – well, go ahead.

Dean: Well, so that is one perjury. Mitchell and Magruder are potential perjurers. There is always the possibility of any one of these individuals blowing. Hunt, Liddy. Liddy is in jail right now, serving his time and having a good time right now. I think Liddy in his own bizarre way the strongest of all of them.

President: Your major guy to keep under control is Hunt?

Dean: That is right.

President: Does he know a lot?

Dean: He knows so much. He could sink Chuck Colson.

President: Don't you think you have to handle Hunt's financial situation damn soon?

Dean: I talked with Mitchell about that last night.

President: It seems to me we have to keep the cap on the bottle that much or we don't have any options.

Questions

1 Who do you think the blackmailers are in the first extract?

2 What are the two men concerned about in the second extract?

3 What actions is Nixon suggesting in the second extract?

4 What exactly do the extracts prove about Nixon's part in the Watergate affair?

5 Why did some Americans find John Mitchell's part in Watergate so shocking?

Acknowledgements

We are grateful to the following for permission to reproduce copyright material:

The Bodley Head & Simon & Schuster Inc. for an extract from 'The Noble Experiment' & 'Konklave in Kokomo' in *The Aspirin Age* ed. Isabel Leighton Copyright © 1949, 1976 by Simon & Schuster Inc.; Chappell Music & Warner Bros Music for the song 'Brother, Can you spare a Dime?' from *Americana*, music by Jay Gorney, words by E. Y. Harburg © 1932 (renewed) Warner Bros Inc., All Rights Reserved; author's agents for extracts from *Pearl Harbour* by Blake Clark; the author, Prof. John H. Clarke for an extract from the short story 'The Boy who Painted Christ Black', Copyright 1940 by John Henrik Clarke, copyright renewed 1968; the author, John Howard Griffin & Houghton Mifflin Co. for extracts from *Black Like Me*, Copyright © 1960, 1961 by John Howard Griffin; Grosset & Dunlap Inc. for an extract from *RN The Memoirs of Richard Nixon*, © 1978 by Richard Nixon; Harper & Row Inc. & author's agents for an adapted & abridged extract from 'Letter from Birmingham Jail, April 16, 1963' from *Why We Can't Wait* by Martin Luther King Jr, Copyright © 1963 by Martin Luther King Jr; Harrap Ltd for extracts from *AHD: The USA in World Affairs* by A. E. Campbell; the author, John Hersey & Alfred Knopf Inc. for extracts from pp. 18, 66, 119 *Hiroshima*, Copyright 1946, renewed 1974 by John Hersey, originally appeared in *The New Yorker*; Alfred Knopf Inc. for extracts from *American Violence: A Documentary History* ed. Richard Hofstadter & Michael Wallace, Copyright © 1970 by Alfred A. Knopf Inc.; Little Brown & Co Inc. & author's agents for extracts from *The Glory and the Dream* by William Manchester, Copyright © 1973, 1974 by William Manchester; Macmillan Publishing Co. Inc. for extracts from *The Other America* by Michael Harrington © Michael Harrington 1962; author's agents & Harper & Row Inc. for extracts from *Richard Nixon: A Political and Personal Portrait* by Earl Mazo, Copyright © 1958 by Earl Mazo; David McKay Co. Inc. for extracts from *America's Immigrants* by Rhoda Hoff, Copyright 1967 by Rhoda Hoff; Orbach & Chambers Ltd for extracts from *No Victory Parades* by Murray Pollner; author's agents & Pantheon Books for extracts from pp. 14–16, 40–3 *Hard Times: An Oral History of the Great Depression* by Studs Terkel, Copyright © 1970 by Studs Terkel; University of Chicago Press for extracts from *Lay My Burden Down* by B. A. Botkin & *Organised Crime in Chicago* ed. J. Landesco, 1929, reprinted 1968 by University of Chicago Press; Webster/ McGraw-Hill Book Co for extracts from *Years of National Turmoil* by James Woodries & R. B. Morris, Copyright 1976; author's agents for an extract from *Upstairs at the White House* by J. B. West © 1973 by J. B. West; author's agents for extracts from *Making of the President* by Theodore White.